Wolf *Empire*

Wolf Empire

An Intimate Portrait of a Species

Scott Ian Barry

THE LYONS PRESS

Guilford, Connecticut

AN IMPRINT OF THE GLOBE PEQUOT PRESS

DEDICATION

*Here's to Raven, Franny and Farley, Charlie Berger
and Aleta . . . and to that joyous celebration between
wolves and humans on a lazy July afternoon.*

The Lyons Press is an imprint of The Globe Pequot Press.

10 9 8 7 6 5 4 3

PRINTED IN CHINA

DESIGNED BY CLAIRE ZOGHB

ISBN 10: 1-59921-053-3
ISBN 13: 978-1-59921-053-7

Library of Congress Cataloging-in-Publication Data is available on file.

To buy books in quantity for corporate use
or incentives, call **(800) 962–0973**
or e-mail **premiums@GlobePequot.com**.

Epigraph

Ours was an empire of sorts
With monarchs and messengers–
Those aspiring on high
And those skimming the depths.
Our mountains were your cities,
Our trees your bastions of tranquility,
Our heavens, your heavens.
All this, and more, within the wolf empire.

—SCOTT IAN BARRY

Contents

Acknowledgments

I would like to express my deepest thanks to Mr. Joel Hecker, of Russo and Burke, who has done more for me than any one hundred people combined. To Holly Rubino and Anne Hawkins, for their professionalism and sensitivity to standing up for what is right. To Chuck Keogh, of Putnam Imaging, for his time-honored artistry, but most importantly, for still believing in "the old ways."

And to Mr. Chris Fricke—my own, private "Lasermeister," at Office Depot in Kingston, New York—for his sublime, even temper in the face of public insanity, ready sense of humor, and sheer wizardry on the Xerox 3535.

My Own Private Empire

I think the one question I've been asked most over the
years has been: "How does a guy from Flushing, Queens,
New York City, end up with *wolves*?"

MY ANSWER HAS ALWAYS BEEN: The fact that I am from New York City made my need for wolves and wilderness that much greater than, say, someone from the suburbs or the country. Looking back, there was something innate, something nearly postnatal that led me to wolves.

As a child, I was a student of the Roman Empire, particularly the myth of Romulus and Remus—how a judicious female wolf came to raise the child who would one day be called, "The Founder of Rome."

I had never believed the all-too-popular scenario for that impish coquette known as Little Red Riding Hood (a tale born out of the superstition of fourteenth-century France). Perhaps I felt this way because of an inquisitive, not to mention rebellious nature. But I simply did not pay attention to the negative "Big Bad Wolf" publicity that was used as a justification to slaughter an entire species.

I had never *known* anyone who had been attacked or eaten by a wolf, or heard any plausible accounts of such. My rationale was: If wolves were such evil creatures, if wolves were such killers . . . then prove it!

I knew that wolves were physically stunning and powerful, and howled hauntingly in the woods. To me, they were better, more fascinating versions of our most beloved pet, the dog.

By the age of five, I found myself inexorably drawn to those qualities. Their sharp-eyed stare—yellow and disarming—and symmetrical, pointed features were the crowning glory of their transcendent inner personas, the physical vehicle for the freedom, strength, and intellect they so forcefully projected.

When my boyhood friends were running about the series of apartment buildings that comprised the Mitchell Gardens complex, in Queens, pretending to be Superman, Batman, or The

Flash, I would often drop down on all fours and become a wolf, a dog, or some mighty predator of the wilderness.

As I grew older, this innocent street-play was at times replaced by the far more ominous theatrics of the street gang, a somewhat ironic endeavor compared with my ongoing studies of the campaigns of Julius Caesar, and the newest interpretations of the Romulus legend (one such interpretation pointing out that in Latin, the word for female wolf is *lupa*—the exact same word for a woman who is a prostitute), giving rise to the theory that the mother of Romulus—who is shown through archaeologic record to have actually existed—might well have been a "woman of the night."

By the age of twelve, I began to psychologically remove myself from the hard, linear confines of Flushing, New York. I began to envision myself, from time to time, as the modern embodiment of the European legend of the "wolf charmer"—a Pied Piper of sorts, a human spirit-figure who lives among packs of wolves in the forests and lakes of the north—he protecting them, they protecting him; he leading them by the hundreds with the mellifluous notes of his wooden flute, over shallow hills, through mist-filled grottos, the wolves multiplying in number as the charmer walks along, surrounded by his adoring beasts.

As with most boys, my teens had become a preoccupation in itself. The difficulties of the "hormone years" and the cultural revolution of the sixties were enough to temporarily put wolves and wolf charmers at the back of my thoughts.

It was not until age seventeen that the beasts and their mythology would reinsinuate themselves into my life. But it was to be an insinuation that would grow to a torrent within me: one that sustains me to this day.

On a clear and brilliant October afternoon, I sat myself down and made the conscious decision to spend the rest of my life surrounded by animals. I got a job as Keeper of the Guard Dogs at a local amusement park. The pay was a pitiful $25 per month, but I was in heaven. I had six new charges in my care: a primitive and sooty-looking former street dog; a monstrous Doberman pinscher; two intimidating, jet-black German shepherds, one of whom would as soon take your arm off as look at you; a frisky but very effective Collie-mix; and for reasons I never quite understood, a handsome Alaskan malamute—a breed not exactly known for its guarding abilities.

But it was that Alaskan malamute, whom I named Ivan, who was to be my bridge to the Wolf Empire.

I began to read about malamutes and their origins. The more information I absorbed, the more I realized that the strongest evidence pointed to this ancient breed (along with the Siberian husky and the Greenland Eskimo dog) being directly descended from wolves. And although there were those who doubted the malamute-wolf genetic connection, there was at the same time a body of information concerning their origins that was so specific, yet so obscure that most people (even those in the field of canid research) were not aware of it.

This information stated that the dog we call the Alaskan malamute today, not only descended from wolves, but from the specific subspecies of *Canis lupus chanco*, or Tibetan wolf—a medium-size, light-pelaged animal from south-central Asia—and that from this subspecies, a domesticated sled dog (the malamute) crossed over the Bering land-ice bridge with the migrations of the native peoples, approximately 35,000 years ago, into western Alaska.

Armed with this knowledge, I was determined not only to be with malamutes, but with wolves as well.

At the age of nineteen, I saw my first wolf. He was an enormous specimen, with cold, sulphur eyes. His head, from the tip of the sagittal crest to the end of his nose, approximated the size of a basketball. His face, which was a beautiful, warm, buff hue with delicate black markings, was framed by an expansive diamond-shaped ruff. He stood on legs that were so sturdy and so tall they resembled the trunks of trees. And his plump, fur-covered paws were so obtrusive, they appeared almost clownish in proportion with the ground beneath them.

The wolf stopped at a distance from me, raised that massive skull, those vacuum-like nostrils, and gleaned the damp air for my scent. I was transfixed, rooted on my shallow piece of Earth, separated from this god by the width of a moderate stream.

With little fanfare, the buff giant lowered his head, then turned around and, with the air of a Herculean dandy, tiptoed away, up the low promontory on which he'd been standing, out of my sight.

For what seemed like an hour, a day, a month, a year—but which I'm sure was only about ten minutes—I lingered on that ridge, re-creating his image, moving up, up, his tabletop-flat backline bouncing gingerly over the piston-like motions of his dense shoulder blades.

Since it is our youthful first impressions in life that stay with us the longest, I have never forgotten the moment that buff wolf-giant stood on the little island-promontory to inspect me, then casually walked away.

He is with me, still.

Two years later, I took my love for wolves to a higher level. I was asked to join the Clem and Jethro Lecture Foundation, which traveled across North America presenting live wolves to the public. The purpose of the tour was to destroy the very myths that myself and an entire generation had been weaned on, and to replace those myths with new, accurate information about the species.

The wolves on tour were *not* pets, or some freakish aberrations of nature. They were, instead, rare individuals who were specifically chosen because of their inherent ability to remain unstressed in the presence of human beings.

If I had been in heaven during my days at the amusement park—well, this must have been heaven to the third power.

In five short years, I had gone from taking care of guard dogs to seeing my first wolf to *living* with wolves on a daily basis.

Yet one year later I was to realize a deeply buried, longtime dream. My lecture colleagues and I were informed that we would be getting a "new member" to our team, and that we were to meet Mori at the Baltimore-Washington Airport (he was due to fly in from California on United Airlines).

We drove directly to the airport, went to the United Air Cargo terminal, and waited. An hour later, the flight arrived. After the last freight package was processed, there stood at the very corner of the shadows a large, rectangular, steel object, reminding me, somewhat ominously, of the alien monolith from the classic sci-fi movie, *2001: A Space Odyssey*.

While my colleagues conversed with the United Air Cargo personnel at the airline counter, I found myself moving toward the rectangle. I did not pause to analyze what I was doing, or why I was doing it. In retrospect, though, I can see myself in the airline hangar . . . walking, walking . . . the stainless steel thing growing larger in my field of vision.

Finally, I stood before it. Taped down to its glinting surface was a bright white-and-orange label that read, *Caution: Live Animal*. And dangling from a small white string on its corner was a tag. I turned the tag over between my fingers. It read, *Mori*.

A profound smile parted my lips. I dropped to my knees and peeked into the shipping crate. All I could see in the darkness between its three metallic bars were two golden orbs, set like distant suns in outer space, staring back at me.

This could mean only one thing—and the breath was taken from my body—that the animal inside was *black*. Jet black. Pure black . . . a pure black wolf!

My greatest, most secret misplaced fantasy had risen from my youth to come true. I was going to be living with a *black wolf*, lecturing with him, teaching with him, *howling* with him. "Ladies and gentlemen," I would tell my lecture audiences, "I would like to present our newest colleague—*Mori*—Mori, the living myth."

In 1976 I left Mori and the lecture tour to stay with friends in Illinois. By August, I was geared for the experience of a lifetime:

I was headed by bus into Canada, to the Quetico Provincial Wilderness in southwestern Ontario Province, where it was estimated 250 wolves lived.

Here was one more irony of my life: I was going to spend five to eight hours per day in a pointed aluminum shell, crossing huge wilderness lakes, searching for wolves, and I didn't even know how to swim.

When asked the obvious question, "What are you going to do if your canoe tips over . . . ?", I'd shrug my shoulders and say, "*Hold on*, I guess."

After the first two weeks in the Quetico, having seen osprey, hawks, bald eagles, moose, loons, and the awe-inspiring northern lights, I was more than ready for wolves, knowing full well how difficult it was to spot them in the wild.

Eight days later—on a damp yet sunny dawn—I was carrying my canoe over my head, up a portage, struggling to balance not so much the weight, but the awkward length of the seventeen-foot Grumman craft.

I gazed down to my left to check my footing, and there, beside my sneaker, were two fresh, wet pawprints. The prints were so fresh and so wet that there was water standing in them. The wolves had to be very close by, perhaps having been there and left, just seconds before I arrived.

I became so excited at the thought of being surrounded by *scores* of wild wolves, that I shouted, "Wolves!" and let go of my canoe, allowing it to bounce on the forest floor, listening to its aluminum skin reverberate through the dense trees and lakes.

I collected my wits, scanned the nearby woods, expecting to see rows of glowing amber eyes observing me. I thought of the wolf-charmer imagery of my youth, and of North American legends about packs of wolves circling the campfires of early explorers.

After trying some of my best howling repertoire and getting no response, I followed the tracks along the left side of the portage. About fifteen yards ahead, the pawprints crossed to the right side of the portage and headed toward a stand of marsh reeds. Just in front of the wolf prints was a set of tracks that told the story: moose; the wolves had been hunting and chased a moose into the marsh, where I had to assume that they either lost it or dove into the pond after it, for there were no other tracks along the portage, farther up, and no signs of a struggle, blood, or a kill on the island.

When I eventually left the Quetico, the memory of my first wolf hunt stayed with me the most. Although the wolves were nowhere to be seen on that particular morning, they had left behind their "signatures," and through those signatures, their legacy to me.

My return to "civilization" was not a pleasant one. I suffered deep cultural shock, having gone from the primordial world of the Quetico Provincial Wilderness to a Burger King in International Falls, Minnesota. I fell into a depression of the mind and spirit that lasted for three months. It seemed I would never recapture the ethereal high I had experienced among wild wolves: the place that I felt I truly belonged; more so, certainly, than among my own kind.

However, on the ninth of September, 1978, I was to take part in one of the most powerful spiritual experiences of my life, at Carnegie Hall, of all places, in New York City.

I had gone back on the road with the wolf lecture tour in May of that year, traveling with two new wolves: Slick, a huge, strawberry-colored and very sweet-natured Alaska male; and Sunny, his trickster brother.

In the past, my colleagues and I had worked closely with renowned musician Paul Winter (of the Paul Winter Consort), presenting our wolves during his uplifting "Earth concerts." I would walk out on stage, after the playing of his instrumental number, "Wolf Eyes," with Mori by my side, speak briefly about wolf mythology, howling, and wolf-sonics, then provide my own "crash course" on how to *realistically* howl like a wolf, and invite the audience to join in.

I always cherished these get-togethers with Paul and his consort, standing with my beloved black packmate, sharing just a small part of our world with the public.

The engagement at Carnegie Hall had been planned well in advance, and a great deal of publicity had been generated for it. We had done local TV and radio shows, brought Slick into the studios in his role as an "ambassador" for wolves and wilderness. So the night of the concert was filled with all the electricity of an Academy Awards gala. Many celebrities had come to be part of this unique event, which had been made even more unique by the presence of my dear friend, Shawn Ogburn, and his magnificent golden eagle, "Briscoe."

At eight p.m. sharp, the lights dimmed. A hush fell over the crowd. The performance began with the lilting notes of Paul's alto saxophone. Five musical numbers later, I heard the haunting, recorded howls that began "Wolf Eyes." In six more minutes, I would be facing a sold-out audience of 2,200 sophisticated, discriminating New Yorkers, attempting to teach them some of the most intimate secrets of wilderness life.

Slick and I came onstage in darkness. Suddenly, we were bathed in the beam of a hot spotlight. The audience gave a collective gasp at the sight of the thirty-one-inch-tall wolf. I began to speak.

Soon, I bid everyone pay close attention to the manner in which wolves howl, pointing out that most times human beings sounded like coyotes with intestinal problems, when they tried to imitate the howl of a wolf.

I proceeded with my crash course. I raised my head toward the upper balcony, contracted my lips, curled back the tip of my tongue (which wolves actually do when howling), and let go a smooth, rising and falling cry.

I noticed an immediate change in Slick's facial expression. The pupils of his eyes dilated. His nostrils expanded. He began tap-dancing in place.

I howled again. To my surprise, the audience began to clap loudly. I asked for quiet, and instructed them to watch Slick.

On my fourth howl, my huge packmate lifted his muzzle toward the roof of Carnegie Hall and released a deep, chilling, single howl that boomed off the acoustic construction of the walls.

. . . Thunderous applause.

I put my finger to my lips, asking for quiet, again.

I howled . . .

Slick howled.

I raised my hand to the crowd, flipped my fingers forward and back, coaxing them to join in.

Now it was my turn to gasp: the standing-room-only crowd burst out with a deafening, droning expression of joy—wailing, howling, *aahhooing* and *ohhing*.

There we were, Slick and I—wolf and human, together—before what felt like the heart of the Earth, the center of the universe. If there is such a thing as palpable love, as tangible goodwill, it was there, that night, at Carnegie Hall in New York City.

I left the road tour that October, after a second emotional high—two standing-room-only lectures at the Smithsonian Institute in Washington, D.C. But I was determined to take my wolf-work one step higher. For me, this meant only one avenue—books.

I felt if I could reach thousands of school students by traveling with live wolves, that with one book alone, I could possibly reach tens of thousands, hundreds of thousands, from my desk.

My first book—a photo-essay, nonfiction work—was called *The Kingdom of Wolves* (G. P. Putnam's Sons). However, it was not until May 1980 that I received a powerful message telling me that writing books was to be my life's calling.

I had moved back to Illinois. On a glorious Monday morning, I went to my mailbox and opened a letter that had originally been addressed to my publisher. In it was a review for *The*

Kingdom of Wolves. I saw that the review had originated in the Northwest Arctic School District, in Kotzebue, Alaska.

Sadly, in some of the places where wolves live, the local residents do not appreciate them. Conversely, in places where wolves have been extirpated, they are often held in high regard. So it was not with the greatest enthusiasm that I began reading this latest review of my book.

To my surprise and delight, the review was very complimentary and labeled the book, "Highly Recommended."

It was at that moment, on the steps of my house in Waukegan, Illinois, that I *knew* I wanted to be an author for the rest of my life. I had no immediate chance of going to Alaska, due to lack of funds and lack of time. Instead, my thoughts and words went for me. My values would be reaching the children, perhaps of the very men who chased and hunted down wolves from airplanes. If *The Kingdom of Wolves* could educate *them* about the species, it could educate a whole generation. . . . And *they* could then educate generations to come.

Here, before me, was the power of the written word; the power of the photographic image.

One month later, in June, I received my first wolf: in other words, a wolf who was legally and technically mine. I have always believed that we can never actually *own* something wild, like a wolf. It would be like saying: "Do you see that cloud, over there? I own it. It's mine."

What arrogance.

Nevertheless, Jalene was donated to me by a zoo in Okla-

Here is Jalene at eight weeks old, and at her adorable best. (Photo by Scott Ian Barry)

homa, specifically for my educational lectures, which I would now be doing under the banner of my own organization, the Wildlife Orientation Lecture Foundation (W.O.L.F.).

I had my first book in print, which was fast becoming a bestseller, and which had been chosen as an "Outstanding Science Trade Book" by the National Science Teachers Association. I was living and lecturing with a wolf that was solely in my care. Things could not be going better.

Jalene and I stop for a brief photo shoot before going to do lectures in St. Louis schools. (Photo courtesy of Aleta L. Pahl)

Or so I thought.

While on tour in Pennsylvania, I looked out the back window of the house I had been staying in, and saw a sight that I should not have seen: an empty space where Jalene should have been.

I stared hard, incredulously, at the spot, as though she would magically appear; as though she would give me her toothy wolf smile, to let me know that everything was fine.

Everything was not fine.

I walked out to the backyard. My beautiful female Alaskan malamute, Copper, who had been traveling with us as a companion and mother figure for Jalene, lifted her head nonchalantly at me, as though nothing out of the ordinary had occurred. This surprised me, because Copper was always very aware of the slightest changes in her immediate environment.

I walked anxiously down the driveway of the house, toward its front yard, then stopped full in place. Lying stretched out like a length of tawny fabric along the ground was Jalene, dead. She had somehow, in some bizarre way (bizarre because I had always taken double and triple precautions to ensure all my animals' safety) gotten loose and run straight into the path of an oncoming truck.

It took many months to get past the shock of Jalene's death. But if the old adage is true, that from the bleakest times can come the best, then the best was yet to come.

On the eleventh of May in the following year, I had another date with destiny—this one at Bradley International Airport, in Hartford, Connecticut.

I remember standing at the open hangar door, the warmth of the evening and the misty spring rain bathing my face. I thought to myself: Most people's children arrive in a hospital, at the hands of a doctor. My "children" come in big metal birds, out of the sky, like the mythical European storks, delivering babies.

At 10:45 p.m., after much pacing in the terminal's waiting room, I spotted the pencil-like silhouette of a Super DC-8 jetliner, descending slowly toward the glistening, black tarmac. It seemed that a profusion of lights dotted the night everywhere: the flashing red-and-green landing lights of the aircraft; the surrealistic blue glow of the runway lights; the lights of the small city in the not-too-far-off distance.

Finally, the Super DC-8 touched down and rolled smoothly toward the deserted hangar, swinging its elegant, fluted nose in my direction. An airline official instructed me to come to his desk to sign shipping papers, where I could wait for my "package."

After watching box after box burst through the conveyor belt hatch into the processing room, a small, white crate with familiar orange lettering pushed through into my section of the arrival area.

I could see a dark shape turning in circles, between the narrow bars of the side window grating. Every now and then there was a flash of pink tongue, a blur of amber from the corner of an eye, a suggestion of tiny, wedge-shaped ears.

The airline official lifted the crate and placed it on the counter before me, then handed me the shipping papers.

"Nice pup," he said, matter-of-factly.

"Thanks," I replied, with a proud paternal smile. Some *pup*, I told myself.

I squeezed the metal latch between my thumb and forefinger. The mesh door swung open. The dark shape *flew* out of the opening and into my arms.

This had to be what fatherhood was like: I was flushed; my skin was hot; I was grinning like a fool, as I cradled the warmth of the little Alaskan tundra wolf against my chest.

I've always told people that my children have four legs. Raven (at seven and a half weeks old) and I share a father-daughter moment at the Klem Road South School in Rochester, New York. (Photo courtesy of Aleta L. Pahl)

Then I thought: Pure black . . . as black as the great northern birds who follow wolf packs for the food of their kills. She flew out of the crate, into my arms.

I will call you "Raven"—Raven the wolf.

The following day, Raven's career as a lecture animal—carrying on the tradition of Slick, Mori, and Jalene—would begin.

I drove with her on my lap, she nestled in a Huggies disposable diaper so that my jeans would not get wet. When I had gone into the local supermarket to buy the diapers I asked myself: Who in the world buys this stuff for a *wolf*? *But*, I realized, a baby is a baby—whether it be wolf, human, or whatever: when they've gotta go, they've gotta go. And go, she did.

Our destination was Boston, Massachusetts, where the next morning, the twelfth of May, I would present Raven in her first program, at an elementary school.

After showing Canadian cinematographer Bill Mason's award-winning film about wolves—*Death of a Legend*—I walked down the main aisle, past children whose eyes were huge with astonishment at the sight of this black chunk with legs.

When we reached the front of the expansive auditorium, I braced Raven beneath her rump in my left arm, then placed the nipple of a plastic bottle filled with Esbilac (simulated bitch's milk) to her lips.

The fact that she was a wolf born in captivity made little difference: she drank as quickly and as hungrily as any of her wild cousins.

When the last of the synthetic milk was gone, I put Raven over my shoulder, gently patted her back several times, and waited till I heard a resounding *bwwaaap*.

First time I ever burped a wolf, I told myself, as six hundred students hooted and clapped and cheered their approval.

We concluded the lectures in Boston, and headed for Rochester, New York, where Raven did her first television appearances.

As the years passed, she grew from a gawky, out-of-proportion pup, to a leggy adolescent, to a stunning adult with silver paws, belly, and chin. In that time, we did concerts with Paul Winter at the Omega Institute in New York, "a.m." morning shows, magazine-format shows, museums, and countless schools.

Anything that can be imagined happening during a live performance—from Raven regurgitating her raw chicken on stage, to me telling a bewildered group of teenagers how "only myself and other wolves" are able to recognize Raven's subtle physical gestures—did happen.

Today, Raven is no longer with me. She is with Mori, Slick, and Jalene. Each day, I stare at their photos, remembering not so much our many triumphs, but the quiet, personal moments we shared. Even death cannot break the intangible bond between human and beast . . . not here . . . not in my own private empire.

If there has been a sum total to my life among wolves, if there has been a single purpose to my endeavors, it would have been just this—that I shared my love for them with others.

And now, as you journey with me into *Wolf Empire*, I share that love with you.

Raven leaves a perfect triangle of untouched fur as she raises her snow-frosted head to look at my camera lens. She is two years old here in her huge enclosure in Woodstock, New York. (Photo by Scott Ian Barry)

Wolf Empire

Siblings

ON A VISIT TO A private wolf preserve in central Vermont, I spotted this stunning white brother and sister. The contrast between them displays a classic case of "sexual dimorphism," or the apparent physical differences between the makeup of the sexes.

Here, the female (left) appears almost doe-like in the gentle sculpting of her muzzle and skull. The notch in her right ear was the result of ever-aggressive blackflies, which literally chewed through her fur and flesh.

The peaceful, attentive male (right) shows a broader, more masculine head with a deeper muzzle at the width of its base.

At one time, it would have been considered "unscientific" or "anthropomorphic" to say that individual wolves looked "masculine" or "feminine." But at least our species has come far enough in its development to finally realize that, yes, wolves are as unique and as different from one another as we are from other humans, and that there are indeed distinct variations in physical appearances of males and females.

THE CLASSIC WOLF

❧ MATURE CANADIAN TIMBER WOLF ❧

ASIDE FROM BEING ONE OF my personal favorites for its air of gentle simplicity, this image holds great sentimental value: It is one of the first photographs I ever took of a wolf.

I had just rounded the bend of a cluster of red pines, when to my amazement I saw this regal male, standing by himself, like a monument carved of fur and bone. His tall legs and long back line, triangular head, and plump paws are all elements that make up the classic wolf.

A good way to think of the species is that to us they look something like dogs; they behave more like cats; and they are built like racehorses.

This adult male displays neither a summer nor a winter coat, but the ever-thickening, even fur of a wolf in early autumn—the crossover period between seasons.

The Rivals

{ Mature Canadian Timber Wolves }

WITH NO LOVE LOST BETWEEN them, these two packmates have reached the point of confrontation.

Although it might appear that the wolf on the left with his bared teeth is the aggressor, he is not. Instead, he is adopting a "submissive-defensive" grin.

If you look closely, you'll notice that he has averted the gaze of his pupils from the wolf on the right, who is actually challenging him with his own "direct stare" and puckered corners of his mouth, as he growls.

While observing the pack, I saw these two wolves constantly challenge and threaten each other. They are also the subjects of the following frame.

The very same behavioral patterns and facial gestures seen here are duplicated in countless situations with our most beloved pet, the domestic dog. In fact, one of the key reasons why children are often bitten in the face by strange dogs is because we, as human beings, naturally encourage eye-to-eye social contact. When applying this behavioral dynamic to interactions between the species—especially children and dogs—the results can be violent and tragic. A dog that receives a prolonged direct stare from a child, at close distance, feels that it has been given nowhere to go, nowhere to find an "escape route" for itself. Its only course of action is to protect itself, and to alleviate the intense stresses thrust upon it; to charge forward and stop the source of the threat.

The pet dog is simply obeying its primal instinct for self-preservation. Unfortunately for the human child, we, as adults, have set him or her up to be the unwitting victim of our own culturally programmed ignorance. When it comes to the great majority of social interactions, both wolves and humans employ visual cues and "trigger mechanisms." Wolves recognize and understand these dynamics, then employ them to create smoother, more functional interactions among the pack. Humans understand these cues in an ultimately less functional way, and because of a lack of knowledge of their immediate purpose and usage, fail to pass them along to their offspring.

Rage

{ Mature Canadian Timber Wolves }

HAVING REACHED THEIR BOILING POINT, the pack members from *The Rivals* have "boiled over."

Even though the visual display here appears quite savage, the entire incident lasted just over a minute. And despite his cruel, pointed teeth, wrinkled muzzle, and fierce eyes, the wolf in the foreground did not further pursue the disagreement; nor was he injured in any way, other than a couple of minor scars.

If you look closely, you will see that the aggressor wolf (left) has a hold of the other wolf by the section of thick fur behind his head, called the "ruff." This, and all parts of the wolf's ruff, not only serve as a windbreak to protect the face, but as protection for the neck, head, and throat against damage caused by predators such as bears or cougars, or by the wolf's far larger, heavier, and more powerful prey such as elk and moose.

The goal of the dominant wolf here is to psychologically intimidate his opponent by physically intimidating him—to "cast him down." For if he actually did serious damage to his rival, there would be one less member of his social-hunting unit—the pack—to help take down prey in order to live another day.

In other words, the wolf pack is only equal to the sum of its parts—to the valuable contributions of each member.

STAR POWER

{ ADULT CANADIAN TIMBER WOLF }

FOR YOUR CONSIDERATION: the blonde-coated female that I call "Kim Basinger," ready for her close-up.

She was the only wolf in the pack without facial markings and with less black mantling in her fur. And she seemed very sweet, the way I picture the famous actress to be.

SYMMETRY

{ ADULT ALASKAN TIMBER WOLF }

THIS DRAMATIC-LOOKING FEMALE DISPLAYS an even symmetry in the graying pattern of her black coat. But this is not why I titled this photo *Symmetry*.

After taking the shot, it dawned on me that she had positioned herself at a nearly identical angle to the layers of the cliff she had climbed upon in order to howl. Such remarkable symmetry is not uncommon in nature (some might say it's just coincidence). Yet it never fails to amaze me when I see it put to such practical use. In this photograph, you can take a ruler, place it roughly at a forty-five-degree angle against the image, and draw accurate parallel lines down the wolf's back, shoulder, neck, and muzzle, then draw more parallel lines at the same angle, across the numerous jagged striations of the cliff.

Perhaps one reason that wolves have managed to survive over the millennia is that they don't pass *through* nature, they become *part of it*.

ARIA

THINK WOLVES ONLY HOWL WITH their lips classically puckered together? Here's proof that they do not.

This intense, black-phase female (approximately 45 percent of wolves in Alaska are "black-phase") is letting fly a potent response to a lone pack member far off in the distance.

It has been my observation that quite often wolves seem to howl along the lines of sexual diversity: that is, females may have what we would think of as "feminine" voices—high, soft, and melodious—while males display deeper, rich, robust tones.

Something Pungent
This Way Comes

{ Adult Canadian Timber Wolf }

WITH THE NEXT SIX FRAMES, I like to think I've created a "wolf mini-movie" of sorts. A lone male picks up the aroma of the Chanel No. 5 perfume that I had laid out early that morning. My choice of perfume was based on random logic. I simply knew that it smelled good to me and was pungent, and that the wolf would definitely go for it. True to all my scent experiments, this male did not become aware of it (even though he was standing directly over the marked area) until a breeze from the west literally carried it to his nose, which then triggered the rolling sequence that follows.

Scientists believe that when a member of the pack comes across the scent of prey, he will rub his body in it, to physically bring back a message to the pack (specifically, the pack leaders) that there is food nearby, and that it is time to go hunting.

Rolling in the scent of prey, or other strong odors, may also *disguise* wolves' body scents—for they also ambush their prey by using boulders, thickets of weeds, or trees as camouflage. Other times, they can be observed walking—almost strolling—among deer, caribou, elk, or buffalo herds, testing for weaknesses in the elderly or very young. Then, when they deem the time is right, they will charge at a thirty-five- to forty-mile-per-hour burst of speed, driving their intended target toward the rest of the pack, who are waiting for the attack.

But the best reason why wolves roll in odors? They *love* to!

WOLF SHUFFLE

❧ ADULT CANADIAN TIMBER WOLF ❧

THE ROLLING SEQUENCE BEGINS AS the male wolf slides the side of his face and neck into the scent.

Like cats, wolves have scent glands located above the eyes, to the sides of their faces, and in the sides of their necks. When they roll in an odor, they are not only taking on that particular aroma; they are also blending their own secretions with it from that specific gland.

When a domestic cat rubs up against its owner, it is not only being affectionate it is also marking its "human parent" as part of its territory.

Bottoms-Up

{ Adult Canadian Timber Wolf }

THE ROLL PROGRESSES AS OUR subject commits himself to the ritual, then rocks onto his back and gathers his paws together, like a puppy at play in the den.

TILT!

COMPLETELY ENGROSSED NOW, THE BIG male covers more of his body as he squirms and shimmies through the scent.

LOST IN SPACE

{ ADULT CANADIAN TIMBER WOLF }

LOOKING LIKE AN INTOXICATED HEDONIST, the pack member momentarily lies still. Soon, he will begin his ritual again.

It has always fascinated me how wolves rolling in odors look so much like domestic cats indulging in catnip. Their facial expressions—glazed eyes, a vacant, distant stare—and body language are very similar. And the apparent "narcotic effect" on both species is nearly identical.

Yet, quite often with wolves, the more putrid the odor, the more they seem to enjoy it.

While on our educational tour across North America many years ago, two of the lecture wolves rolled in dead fish. I asked myself, "How can these guys *stand* that smell, all over them, and be able to tolerate it in their noses?"

I finally came to realize that wolves operate on a different "olfactory value system" than we do. What may smell perfectly awful to us may be a slice of heaven to them.

ECSTASY

{ ADULT CANADIAN TIMBER WOLF }

IN THIS SIXTH AND FINAL frame of the *Something Pungent This Way Comes* rolling sequence, our intrepid subject is in full revelry, as he pitches onto his back, wriggles frenetically across the scent, then kicks and jerks his legs into the air.

Whether this otherwise dignified male knew it or not, he was helping to prove a point that I have been making for a long time now: that, simply put, wolves can be very *silly*, playful creatures.

Movie Star

{ Adult Canadian Timber Wolf }

WHEN I FIRST CAPTURED THIS head study of the pack leader, I felt that he was so handsome, so perfect in facial proportion and symmetry—a virtual Hollywood version of what it is to be a wolf—that I decided to call him "Cary Grant."

He is the only wolf I've ever seen—out of one hundred—that did not have yellow eyes, or brown eyes, or eyes with shades of gold. Rather, he had pale, lime-green eyes that showed like muted headlamps within the angular features of his face.

In the three-quarter turn of his head here you can see the perfect outline and texture of his diamond-shaped ruff, the perfect balance between the length of his muzzle and his skull, the balance between his wedge-shaped ears and the breadth of his forehead, and the serene, confident gaze of a true "alpha."

Like most pack leaders (who have received the very best nutrition, as their status dictates), he had the most robust winter coat and was in the best overall condition.

In deference to the demands of our current pop culture, I suppose that I am going to have to rename him "George Clooney."

Sorry, Cary.

Sculpted in White

{ Adult Alaskan Timber Wolf }

IF "CARY GRANT," THE LEADER of the Canadian Pack, is my poster boy for "male wolfdom," then, certainly, this gorgeous creature is the poster girl for "female wolfdom."

Everything about her visage—from her chiseled, triangular muzzle, to her petite, wedge-shaped ears and diamond-configured ruff, to her searching, oblique eyes—speaks to her ultimate femininity, strength, and adherence to the dictates of sexual dimorphism.

Unlike the family dog, the angle of the wolf's eye—or orbital socket—falls into a range of forty to forty-five degrees, giving it that characteristic "sharp-eyed stare." In contrast, the angle of the dog's orbital socket falls into a less acute range of fifty-three to sixty degrees—the product of genetic selection by human beings—otherwise known as "domestication . . ."

If you look closely at the wolf in this photo, you will see the notch carved out of the top of her right ear by blackflies, which tells us that this is the same female from *Siblings*.

Getting Mushy
and Get Lost, Kid!

{ Mixed-Age Canadian Timber Wolves }

A VERY SOLICITOUS YOUNGER MALE approaches a dominant elder pack member in a classic case of "active submission." He is actively casting himself into a low physical posture; his eyes are beginning to draw back into slits; his ears are flattened firmly against his head; and he is thrusting his tongue toward the elder wolf—all prominent displays that simulate, or ritualize, the actions of young pups beseeching their parents for food or attention.

However, in this case, the elder wolf *also* seems to be displaying submissive behavior. His ears are pressed against his skull; his tongue gently pokes out, through his lips, at the other wolf; and if you look closely at the wolves' faces, you will see that neither one is actually making eye contact with the other. They are both casting their gazes away, so as to avoid the classic challenge of a "direct stare."

Yet all this does not necessarily signify that the elder wolf is being submissive. For as I continued to watch these two males interact, the true story revealed itself.

After receiving the younger wolf's solicitations of respect and affection with an equally social greeting, the elder male (left) gradually loses patience. In the blink of an eye, he flashes his thorny white teeth and seizes the muzzle of the other animal, saying in his own way, "Get lost, kid! Enough is enough."

Although the younger wolf is grimacing slightly, with his muzzle wedged between the elder's jaws, the impression of drama and implied violence here is a false one. This seemingly aggressive behavior lasted only seconds, and was more powerful with its disciplinary statement than it was in any physical damage done.

The one tip-off or giveaway that this incident is nothing more than a benign moment in the life of the pack is the expression—or lack thereof—on the face of the supine pack member at the far left.

If this had been a more dramatic, or pack-threatening situation, this third wolf would have displayed raised hackles (the fur along a wolf's shoulders and backline), an erect tail, erect ears, and a direct stare of the eyes, with a "concerned" facial expression. Instead, his expression says, "This is no big deal."

Conserving Heat

{ Mature Canadian Timber Wolf }

JUST LIKE YOUR FAMILY DOG, a wolf will curl himself into a ball in cold weather, except that wolves did it first—some two million years before the domestic dog.

This alert male is not only conserving body heat with his circular configuration; he is actually promoting the *production* of body heat.

Had the weather conditions in this photo been more severe, the wolf would have curled himself even tighter, and wrapped the end of his long brush tail completely around his nose and face to protect them. When a wolf curls up, he is compressing muscle mass, drawing his body as a whole into a tighter configuration of fur—like one solid unit that also closes down blood vessels to raise the body's overall temperature, or at least to maintain it.

For years, scientists could not understand why the pads on the bottoms of wolves' paws, or their noses and the tips of their ears, did not freeze solid in critical sub-zero temperatures, since these are the body's most vulnerable extremities.

In the 1970s—in horrendous experiments done at the Naval Arctic Research Lab in Point Barrow, Alaska—scientists submerged wolves' feet into cold acid to test their theories on the wolf's system of "heat exchange." They discovered that the wolf's blood vessels constricted, or "shut down" to their extremities, so that the rich oxygen supply would not be allowed to escape: would not be allowed to "aerate," or cool down the ears, nose, and feet. Otherwise, the tops of the wolf's ears could freeze solid, then snap off, in conditions far below zero Fahrenheit.

Ironically, this same curled-up position is used in hot weather, to protect the wolf's extremities from onslaughts of aggressive blackflies and mosquitoes.

A Wolf-Pack Portrait

{ Canadian Timber Wolves of Mixed Age and Gender }

I HOLD THIS PHOTO VERY close to my heart. It is one of my most well-known images, having been seen in magazines, books, newspapers, and splashed across the television screen on NBC's *Today Show*.

I was lucky enough to be in the right place at the right time, when these packmates simultaneously gathered at the crest of a small hill to watch the movements of white-tailed deer in a shallow glen below.

The group from left to right, on top, are all older pups, approximately eight months old. The fellow at the far right is most likely a two-year-old adolescent sibling—judging by his larger size and more mature expression.

After watching the wolf on the lower left, I believe she is the mother of the pups or at least an aunt. She has an obviously close relationship with the pups, and is one of two possible breeding-age females in the pack. Since she is also the alpha female, it would be safe to conclude that she is the mother of these older pups.

Wolf packs are "families" in every sense of the word—just as much as human families—except with several major differences: Wolves don't get divorced. They don't abuse or abandon their children. And they don't go on television talk shows, spilling their guts about their failed relationships to other wolves.

TÊTE-À-TÊTE-À-TÊTE

{ Mixed-Gender Canadian Timber Wolves }

CHANEL NO. 5, hard at work.

Under Construction

{ Mature Canadian Timber Wolves }

IN THE PAST, MOVIES AND television documentaries have depicted wolves building dens in powdery, soft earth, suggesting that this activity is *always* performed in balmy, springlike weather. Heavier snow often remains in many wolf territories until early May, especially in northern latitudes. This means that the beginnings of many den sites would have to be undertaken in at least semi-frozen ground, and under snowy conditions. Wolf pups are usually born in their dens from late March to late May, depending on the latitude. The higher the latitude, the later the warming cycle, and thus, the later the birthing process.

The female will gradually "remodel" her den for several weeks, then she may complete her work a week or two before giving birth, all the while performing last-minute "touch-ups."

The primary role of the den is to serve as a birth chamber and refuge for newborn pups of the alpha female. The den then becomes the center of pack life for the first three months after the pups are born. At four months, the entire pack will move to an open-air terrain, protected by trees, called a "rendezvous site."

In order to keep large predators, such as bear, from entering the den and stealing or eating the pups (sometimes, right there before the parents' eyes), den entrances are usually made no wider than two feet across, and only thirteen to eighteen inches high. This means that the parents of the pups must first crouch low to enter the birth area.

Wolf dens can be as shallow as seven feet deep, and as extensive as thirty feet deep, with side chambers and specific activity areas. In general, though, dens average about ten to twelve feet deep. They may be built into hilltops, beneath logs, expanded from old fox dens, or the dens of other wolves. Some dens are used by the same pack for many years; some are used once, then never again. And some—like the image in this photo—are built side-by-side, next to already-existing dens.

About two weeks before the female is ready to give birth, the father of the pups, or other pack members, begin to bury caches of meat within close range of the den site, so that the mother of the pups can either reach a quick food source for herself, or so that food can be brought to her.

Quite often, no wolf will be allowed to enter the den in the first two weeks after the pups are born—not even the father. The female is in control during this time—truly the "queen of her castle."

Foxy Lady

{ ADULT FEMALE OF UNKNOWN ORIGIN }

ALTHOUGH I NEVER DID KNOW precisely what type of wolf this beautiful "biscuit-colored" female was, she struck me as having refined, features that were more "vulpine" (foxlike) than "lupine" (wolflike).

In the field of wolf taxonomy in North America, the Gray Wolf and Red Wolf are the two major species recognized. Gray Wolves are not necessarily "gray" in shading or color; and Red Wolves are not necessarily "red."

As we have seen throughout these pages, variation is the key to survival. Wolves, though born predominantly black, dark gray, or dark brown, can have coat colors that range from pure black to pure white, with gradations of tan, buff, brown, biscuit, yellow, pale gray, medium gray, charcoal, or any combination of the above.

There are twenty-four recognized subspecies of Gray Wolf in North America, and approximately three recognized subspecies of red wolf (the smaller, southern-latitude species).

My problem with this system is twofold. First, many of the wolf's subspecies are classified by *our own* geographic boundaries. For example, the eastern timber wolf's westernmost boundary lies just within the Canadian province of Manitoba. If members of that subspecies travel a long distance and end up, say, in the Rocky Mountains, do they then become Northern Rocky Mountain wolves? To the best of my knowledge, wolves still do not recognize arbitrary human political boundaries. Second, if members of these subspecies, who live near the boundaries where the next subspecies exist, cross over and interbreed with that other subspecies, then how do we classify the resulting offspring?

Which leads me to an even more valid argument: a number of the "scientifically classified" wolf subspecies are based on a pitifully small number of physical specimens. The "Banks Island wolf" is literally based on two skins and one skull for its classification—not much of a scientific sample to name an entire subspecies, if you ask me. And the Melville Island and Ellesmere Island subspecies are also based on a woefully small number of physical specimens from these areas.

The only reason for naming these particular subspecies is the fact that they were at least found on their specific, geographic locations. For the sake of accuracy and simplicity, there should probably be only fifteen or so actual subspecies of gray wolf recognized or classified in North America, only those that can be directly attributed to obvious and specific geographic or topographic locations: the Rocky Mountain wolf, the Great Plains wolf, the Hudson Bay wolf, and so on.

But the most accurate and simplest classification of all is to call all these subspecies "wolf."

Madonna on Guard

❧ Iranian Wolf Mother and Pup ❧

THE FOLLOWING TWO-FRAME SEQUENCE is a rare one for two reasons: the subjects of the photos belong to the subspecies of gray wolf (*Canis lupus pallipes*) or "Iranian wolf." And the pup featured in both frames is only eleven days old.

Here, the mother raises her head in response to a noise in the distance. She projects a vigilant stare, as she shelters her baby in the crook of her body. If she determines the noise to be a threat, she will pick up her pup in her mouth—across the width of its back, or over the top of its head—and move it to a safer location.

Although wolf pups can fairly well regulate their body heat at about eight weeks old, it will not be until they are three to four months of age that they can fully regulate their heat exchange system. This pup is completely dependent on its mother for food, warmth, and protection.

Notice the prominent frontal lobe (the rounded protrusion above her eyes) of the mother's skull, and how it contrasts with the slightly flatter profile of the North American wolves (except for the Rocky Mountain gray wolf, which also features a prominent frontal lobe).

Due to the hot, dry climate in which this subspecies lives, the coat of the Iranian wolf is shorter and less dense than the fur of wolves from North America, Northern Europe, and Northeast Asia. But the purpose of the coat, in this case, is to dissipate heat as efficiently as possible, away from the body, in the searing deserts of the Middle East.

Madonna at Rest

{ Iranian Wolf Mother and Pup }

GRADUALLY, THE IRANIAN WOLF MOTHER determines that there is no cause for alarm. She lowers her head to the ground and rests as her young one snuggles higher against her body.

At eleven days old, this pup's eyes have not yet opened. In another three days or so, its eyelids will part, but it will be unable to focus its vision clearly for several weeks. In another eight to ten days, it will begin to hear.

HEADS-UP

{ IRANIAN WOLF MOTHER AND PUP }

IN THIS FINAL FRAME OF the Iranian wolf grouping, we see visual evidence (a rather rare example) of the mother wolf actually picking up her pup by its head to move it to a new location.

Although it may appear so, the pup is in no way being hurt. It instinctively goes limp, which allows its mother to grasp it firmly but gently between her jaws in the exact way that we see female cats sometimes pick up their kittens.

Since there was no real danger presented here, and since this method of carrying the pup is not quite as efficient as carrying it by its back, the Iranian wolf matriarch did not take her child very far away—just deeper into the brush.

One day, in the not-too-far-off future, the grown-up pup will carry her own offspring in this same manner, continuing the wolf's cycle of efficient child-rearing for years to come.

The Warrior

{ Mature Canadian Timber Wolf }

PONDERING SOMETHING THAT ONLY WOLVES would keep between themselves, this adult male pack member displays various scars and tooth punctures along the bridge of his muzzle and upper corner of his forehead: remnant tokens of his battles with his nemesis from *The Rivals* and *Rage*.

As I have described in my books and lectures over the years, more often than not, wolf disputes within a pack—though sometimes looking and sounding horrendous—produce nothing more than minor punctures, cuts, and scars, but no major damage.

As seen in fights between domestic dogs, some of the worst damage is done relatively quietly, often when ritualized displays and communications were not employed to vent rising aggressions.

The one incident during which I saw a wolf actually kill another wolf took place during the breeding season (mid-January to mid-March), when wolves go through a substantial hormonal change.

The incident occurred very quickly, and completely silently. The *subordinate* female approached the alpha female, and challenged her by invading her personal space. When the alpha female responded with growls and a strong direct stare, the subordinate seized her by the throat, and methodically crushed the alpha's trachea between her molar teeth at the back of her mouth. The alpha female immediately went into shock, and soon died.

Thereafter, I always called this event "The Silent Death."

A Moment in Time

{ Mature Canadian Timber Wolves }

TWO PACKMATES HAVE AWAKENED FROM sleeping out a snowstorm and have shaken themselves dry as they prepare to head deeper into their territory.

The female (foreground) shows a definitely more refined head, muzzle, and body than her male counterpart. I estimate her weight to be about sixty pounds, and the male's, about eighty-five to ninety pounds.

Wolves can weigh as little as forty-five pounds—common in the red wolf species and the Mexican gray wolf subspecies—and up to about one hundred and fifty pounds, as seen in the enormous males who inhabit the Interior of Alaska, the Yukon Territory in northwest Canada, eastern Siberia, and the Mackenzie Delta in Canada's Mackenzie District.

Perhaps the largest wolf ever discovered (depending on which biologist's account you choose to accept) came from central Alaska. He weighed an impressive one hundred seventy-five pounds, and stood forty-two inches tall at the shoulders.

Your Place, or Mine?

{ Adult Canadian Timber Wolf }

THIS IS ONE OF THOSE RARE anecdotes that falls into the category of "You can't make this stuff up."

The subject of this photo is the female I called "Kim" (seen earlier in *Star Power*). The time is late January—in the midst of the wolf breeding season.

On a mercifully mild afternoon, I'd been observing the pack since early morning. I watched the packmembers go through their daily cycles of rest, play, and minor disagreements, and, since it was the mating time, their "soap opera" interludes.

This particular episode of "As the Wolf Turns" had Kim soliciting the pack leader to mate with her—even though she was a relatively low-ranking female; even though the alpha female could have knocked the tar out of her (as will be seen in *Pressure!*)

But determined, deprived Kim "wanted her man." She continued to pester the alpha male, even though he turned a cold shoulder to her; even though she squeaked and whined in high, solicitous pitches, nuzzled up against him, and licked at his face. No dice.

I watched the pretty blonde female plod miserably to the crest of the pack's favorite hill, opposite me, then suddenly glance back over her shoulder, in my direction. I quickly snapped the photo you see here. After whining and moaning some more—as though begging a form of redemption that could not be hers—Kim slowly descended the hill. She did not seek out the alpha male. She did not walk away. She did, in fact, move straight in my direction until she stood on the snowy banks of the inlet, just across from me. Despite the fact that my brain was nearly bursting with the once-in-a-lifetime significance of this moment, I remained calm.

Now, with a renewed zeal, she whimpered and squeaked right at me! But this was not the tragic keening of before. This was the precise delivery of hope and enthusiasm that she had shown to the alpha male.

Amazing, I told myself. But it was not as amazing as what was to come. With a single-minded deliberation, Kim turned slowly around and pointed her backside straight at me. Just as ceremoniously, she swept her long tail to her left and exposed her genitalia. No longer squeaking and whining, she just stared at me. Finally, she began swishing her entire rump left-to-right, then right-to-left, over and over. And I, utterly incredulous, immediately knew the outlandish meaning of this event: A *wolf*, a wild creature, was gesturing for me to *mate* with her! What made this incident so singularly spectacular was that a wolf thought of me, in every way, shape, and form, as *one of her own kind*.

Till the day I die, I will be given no greater compliment, no greater validation, than Kim's "gift" to me on that January afternoon.

It's a Bird! It's a Plane! It's . . .

❧ Mature Canadian Timber Wolf ❧

. . . A SQUIRREL!

After the breeding season has ended, Kim intensely watches the manic behavior of a black-phase squirrel. She rushes her quarry and chases it up a tree. The nails of her front left paw are fully extended as she digs them into the back of the red pine to keep her balance.

Wolves are incredibly aware animals—much more so than our kind. Very little gets past them. In fact, I have often told lecture audiences and the media, "You can't trick a wolf more than once."

Once they have learned a new, or specific behavior—usually by trial and error—they will then incorporate that behavior into their everyday lives.

One of the best examples of this concept occurred in the late 1970s. A white, female wolf, named Virginia, kept secretly escaping from the Los Angeles Zoo. She roamed the streets, sometimes joining up with packs of dogs, sometimes keeping to herself—all the while taking "goodies" from local garbage cans.

Virginia was eventually recaptured and put back into her enclosure at the zoo. One particular day, the keeper came for her daily feeding, and *surprise*—no Virginia!

Eventually, she was captured again. Several months later, she was gone. An alert zookeeper noticed that there were "claw marks" going up the bark of the tree, at the far corner of the enclosure. Virginia the wolf had *climbed* out.

Pressure!

IN A NEARLY IDENTICAL BEHAVIORAL scenario to *The Rivals*, two pack-mates—Kim (right) and the alpha female—confront each other on a sandy slope. Except here the ritualized aggression is enhanced by fully engaged body postures.

Though Kim savagely bears her teeth and wrinkles the bridge of her muzzle, she has cast herself low, with flattened ears, pulled-back lips, and a tail that is firmly tucked beneath her rump to protect her genital area. It is an exhibition learned during puppyhood, another ritualized avoidance of true violence.

The alpha female projects a tall posture and erect tail—the classic dominant signals. And like the dominant wolf in *The Rivals*, she, too, has puckered the corner of her muzzle. She, too, is growling.

Yet there is an odd dynamic going on here: If you look very closely—or use a magnifying glass—you will see that "Kim" is projecting a strong direct stare at her tormentor, while the alpha female is actually *avoiding* the subordinate wolf's defiant attempt to protect herself. Which proves an old adage: Put too much pressure on a rival, and it just may backfire on you.

Surveillance

{ Mature Canadian Timber Wolves }

TWO MALES RISE TO a high point within their territory, in the midst of a gently falling snow. They are surveying their domain for threats, such as bear, cougar, or alien wolves; or for possible sources of food, such as deer, moose, beaver, elk, or rabbit. If they spot prey, they will return to the pack to engage them in the hunt.

As with most wolves, these handsome packmates clearly favor hilltops, ridges, and slopes, where they can have an extended, open view, and an obvious advantage in the presence of danger.

However, there is one more reason why wolves seek out high places, perhaps the best reason of all: They simply enjoy being up high.

SHADOWEYE

{ MATURE CANADIAN TIMBER WOLF }

TO MY MIND, NOTHING IN this world quite conveys the powerful dynamic between shadow and light, like black-and-white photography.

This intensely alert male seems to stand at the threshold between two planes of existence—the harsh reality of the light, and the ethereal lack of substance, in the void of shadows. His cold, amber eye appears like a stark marble that punctuates the sharp-spire markings of his face.

I cannot speak for the void of shadows, but in the real world, this golden light has been given different names around the planet. My favorite is "Ross's Light," named after the eighteenth-century Canadian explorer who described this beautiful and moody curtain-fall to his wilderness days.

FRONT PAW

{ CANADIAN TIMBER WOLF }

THIS DEEPLY ETCHED FRONT PAW print from a mature wolf could have been sculpted by Leonardo da Vinci himself, so pure is it in preserving the exact moment of impact by its creator.

Over the years, I've come upon a method for determining a wolf's weight—and therefore, its height—by placing my gently closed fist just above the print. Whenever the width of the print extends slightly past the sides of my hand, the wolf proves to be somewhere around one hundred pounds, and between twenty-seven and twenty-nine inches tall at the shoulders.

I have had the opportunity to do this experiment many times—both in the wild and in captivity. Obviously, captive situations provide greater access for measuring paw prints and wolf sizes.

Each time I used this method to measure our lecture wolves' paw prints, then went through the challenging ritual of weighing them, the degree of accuracy was very high.

Of course, if you're tracking wild wolves in soft, slushy snow, you must question the accuracy of measuring the footprints in this manner. For when the snow begins to melt and grows even softer, the wolf's paw print will expand with it, and give the false impression that you are hot on the heels of a lupine giant. Proving once again, that nature—ever the trickster—is more clever than we are.

Rear Paw

{ Canadian Timber Wolf }

HERE, THE PERFECT IMPRINT OF a wolf's rear paw (center) splits a front paw print in half. Other paw prints surround this exquisite signature, detailing an area of heavy wolf activity.

Notice that the top two nail impressions angle *inward* toward an imaginary centerline. This tells us that the rear paw's configuration is "oval" in the vertical sense, and is a *right* rear paw.

The close grouping of the nails also tells us that the rear paws of wolves are narrower than the front paws, and therefore do not need to expand to support or distribute most of the animal's weight, as the front paws do.

Unlike horses—which must often be put to sleep when sustaining injuries to their legs because they rely too greatly on them to support their body weight—wolves can, and sometimes do, survive on three legs.

Venerated

{ Adult Canadian Timber Wolf }

WITH HER HOLLOWED AND ROUNDED left eye, worn ear-tips, and lack of markings, the wise, benevolent, yet somewhat sad face of an elderly female speaks volumes.

She may be as old as twelve or thirteen years, which in the wild is not very common. Wild wolves must struggle to survive. They are shot, poisoned, trapped, burned within their dens by human beings. They die largely of malnutrition, parasites, and starvation. All these factors, and more, limit their lives to eight to ten years.

In captivity, these stresses are mainly eliminated, and wolves may reach sixteen years of age or more. This does not mean, however, that we need *any* *more* wolves in captivity. For if there is one place where the species belongs and must thrive, it is in the wild: in the mountains, the tundra, the forests, the plains, the swamps and marshlands. This is the wolf's birthright; and these are the areas that wolves call *home*.

For the elder female in this photo, luck was on her side to have lived so long. She was, in fact, a venerated member of her pack.

Throughout human history—particularly in the ancient cultures of China, Japan, Greece, Rome, Israel, India, and the Americas—the elder members of society were revered for their knowledge and life experience. Only in modern Judeo-Christian culture have the old ones been disregarded and discarded.

Just one more lesson that we can learn from wolves.

I May Be Old—But I'm Not Dead!

{ Adult Canadian Timber Wolf }

HERE, FOR YOUR APPROVAL, IS the elder female from *Venerated*, in a somewhat less cordial mood.

I found it amusing, and heartening, that the old girl was able to project such a fierce display at two pack members who kept frolicking and bouncing around her, while she simply wanted to be left alone to sleep.

Maybe the fact that the pack leader was lying right beside her had something to do with a boost in her confidence, or maybe at her age she had the right to be literally "bitchy."

Getting to Know You

⁞ Adult Canadian Timber Wolf ⁞

IN A THIRD, COMPLETELY DIFFERENT look at the pack member from the previous two photographs, the elder female casts herself down in a classic example of passive submission as the alpha female approaches.

The term *passive submission* connotes exactly what it sounds like: the subordinate wolf lies perfectly still, perfectly passive, and presents herself to the dominant female for inspection.

No one knows precisely what percentage of female wolves become "pack leaders" in wolf society. But the percentage is low. Approximately one out of twenty packs may have a "female alpha."

Within the typical pack structure, the alpha female often ranks just below her alpha male mate (the pack leader). One way in which a high-ranking female can become leader of the pack is to assume or fill the position of her male mate if he dies.

Whenever I have seen this circumstance unfold before me, the alpha female/pack leader turned out to be just as dominant (if not more so) as her mate.

Many wolf packs, though, maintain a two-tiered social structure: a ranking of male members and a parallel ranking of female members. This sort of separate-but-equal system blends together each day when the members of the pack interact.

Ironically, there is an expression that applies to both wolves and Alaskan malamute sled dogs, which to my mind, has proven itself to be true over the past thirty-three years that I've observed wolves: "Males fight for status. Females fight to kill."

Make Your Mark in the World

{ Adult Canadian Timber Wolf }

ON A CLEAR, SUNNY MORNING in March, the alpha female of the pack squats low to mark her territory from the crest of a snowy hill. Each wolf in the pack has a slightly different odor to his or her urine. When a strange wolf or another predator nears a pack's borders, it can tell how many members reside there by cataloguing through its olfactory membranes the number of varied scents that have been left at the base of trees, rocks, shrubs, mounds of earth, snow, food caches, or den sites.

These physically marked areas then become known as "scent posts," which are refreshed each day by members of the pack, and which help serve as warnings to intruders to *stay out*.

If a pack has abandoned its territory, the scent posts will gradually weaken, then fade, leaving a new message to alien wolves and other predators—"The road ahead is safe. No one lives here anymore. You may enter now."

What I like most about this image of a vigilant alpha female is the pure projection of power from her shoulders and thighs. The dense musculature in these two areas forms perfect ovals beneath her fur. And the tightly sprung, forty-five-degree angle of her body gives her the look of a dart, ready to fly.

Serenity

{ Adult Canadian Timber Wolf }

HERE, ONCE MORE FOR ITS sense of utter peace and self-containment, is the image of a wolf sublimely asleep.

This large, elder male has lost the markings and darker coat of his youth. Though he is still capable of killing in the hunt, and engaging in the commotion that can characterize the social interactions of the pack, I noticed while I observed him over a period of ten years that he increasingly preferred his time alone, beneath the reaching limbs of the snow-laden boughs.

I felt a twinge of sorrow for him, for the days of his life that had long gone by. Yet at the same time, I truly admired him for having come this far: for having reached the approximate age of ten years old, with his health and his dignity intact.

Perhaps in his personal serenity, he had come to know the secrets of the universe, secrets that our kind has long forgotten.

In Your Face, Baby

⸢ Mixed-Age Canadian Timber Wolves ⸥

I SUPPOSE YOU COULD THINK of this photo as the ultimate example of getting "up close and personal." The mature male on the right is obviously making his point to the older pup on the left. This is classic Wolf 101 textbook behavior when it comes to discipline—except here, we actually get to see the adult's lower left canine tooth sinking into the fur of the pup's muzzle, and the full flattening of the pup's ear against his head.

As I've said earlier, this experience is only momentarily painful for the young wolf. His tightly shut eye represents the social and psychological effects of the adult's discipline more than any imagined harm.

And speaking of that canine tooth, I feel compelled to point out that the word we use—"canine"—for wolves, dogs, coyotes, and foxes in North America is actually a misnomer. Canine derives from the Latin *"canidae"*—the *actual* name for the family of wolves, dogs, coyotes, and foxes. When the "ae" is removed from *canidae*, we are left with the term we use to classify the species today: "canid."

So the family that includes wolves, dogs, coyotes, and foxes is properly referred to in the twenty-first century as the "Canid Family."

To call a wolf a *canine* is pretty much the same as calling it a "tooth," such as a bicuspid or a molar.

A wolf is *not* a tooth. He or she is a "Canid."

Eye to Eye

{ Adult Eastern Timber Wolf }

ALTHOUGH EUROPEAN FOLKLORE HAS ALWAYS made much of the wolf's yellow eyes, the brown-eyed stare of this handsome eastern timber wolf male shows the diversity in the species. It is also possible to find wolves with one yellow eye and one brown eye, but not blue, as blue is linked to domestic gene pools.

An obscure North American myth claims that wolves whose eyes flare red when struck by a source of light at night are "crazed," or highly aggressive; and wolves whose eyes flare green are sane and benign. This, of course, is nonsense—mere mythology. Wolves, along with other predatory mammals, possess a cellular layer of tissue called the *tapetum lucidum* (Latin for illuminated tapestry).

When the light from a campfire, flashlight, or car beam strikes a wolf's eye, it passes through the pupil, then through the retina, and strikes the *tapetum lucidum*, which flares the light back to ocular receptors, and illuminates the eye. This biomechanism also allows the wolf to see more clearly and more efficiently in the dark.

The fact that a wolf's eyes flare red or green has nothing at all to do with the individual's level of sanity or personality. It is simply the angle and intensity of the light source that determines this chromatic illumination.

You can prove this to yourself at home. Shine a flashlight beam at your family pet. As the angle of the beam shifts, so too will your dog or cat's shade of reflected eye color. More direct, intense light will usually produce a green-eye effect. Conversely, a lower angle and less intense light will produce a red-eye effect.

And I'm willing to bet that your pet will remain sane throughout the experiment.

Which Way Did They Go?

{ Adult Canadian Timber Wolves }

ALTHOUGH APPEARING SOMEWHAT CASUAL, once again the pack is ever alert, as they gaze across their territory in three different directions.

Kim, in the foreground, appears particularly watchful.

Researchers have theorized over the years that it is the lowest-ranking wolves, or "omegas" (who may be more on-edge, or more defensive and protective of themselves due to their less solid standing in the pack), who make the best guardians of wolf society. But it has been my experience, through the decades, that this is not necessarily so.

Once again, the individual personality of any given pack member plays the greatest part in his or her watchfulness.

I have witnessed omega wolves act as lookouts for the pack's safety. And I have witnessed assertive alpha wolves fill the role of guardians (precisely for the opposite reason of the "omega theory") because the alphas were confident, dominant personalities, whose natural inclinations were to get out there and defend their families.

But if seeing is believing, the next two images provide evidence of two *middle-ranking* pack members working together to keep a vigilant watch over their territory.

The Sentinels

{ Mature Canadian Timber Wolves }

ON THE SAME GLOOMY, OVERCAST afternoon as in *Peekaboo*, these two middle-ranking males (roughly twenty-eight inches tall at the shoulders, and ninety pounds) emerged from the distant woods, crossed a level expanse of terrain, then stopped short to assume their watchful positions.

Perhaps the snow that began to fall muffled my senses, for I could not see or hear what it was they were guarding against.

What I found most interesting about "Butch and Sundance," as I enjoyed calling them, was that they always hung out together, worked as a team, and played together. My suspicion, though, is that Sundance, on the right, was the more dominant of the two.

A Single Purpose

THE SNOW HAS BEGUN TO fall harder. And perhaps because of it—as though on some silent, secret cue—Butch and Sundance turn and face the potential, distant threat together.

Over the millennia, there has always been success and safety in numbers for wolves. This is certainly the case for these two middle-ranking males, who, in their particular pack structure, have collectively assumed the role of lookouts.

Individually, though, they were not as protective of their borders. But their collective cooperation actually helped both of them maintain their status quo in the middle of the pack's social strata—never rising to an alpha position, yet never falling to omega ranking.

And as for whatever it was they had decided to stand guard against, I never found it. After a while, they turned in unison and walked back across the open terrain, back into the trees.

Statuesque

{ Mature Canadian Wolf }

THIS STRIKING FEMALE IS A member of the *Canis lupus occidentalis* subspecies, or Mackenzie Valley wolf from the Northwest Territories of Canada. Along with *Canis lupus pambasileus*, the Interior of Alaska wolf, they make up some of the tallest wolves in the world.

She displays the classically large paws and long, tapered skull characteristic of the subspecies. Her elegant, reaching legs brought her to a height of approximately twenty-nine inches tall at the shoulders, which means that she weighed in the neighborhood of ninety to one hundred pounds. Now, that's a big girl!

Get 'Im!

{ Young Canadian Timber Wolves }

THESE FOUR PUPS—APPROXIMATELY SIX months old—are hard at play. The pup on the far right receives the action from his littermates with a somewhat fierce display, as they "assault" him in unison. His ears are very erect, and pitched forward; he projects a strong direct stare at the pup before him; his muzzle is wrinkled; and his teeth are partially bared.

But his show of bravado is actually a ruse. He has betrayed his true status in this friendly melée, with his prominently raised right front paw—a gesture of solicitation and uncertainty—in the same manner a child might push away a schoolyard bully with his outstretched hand, solely to defend himself.

The wolf at the rear left also shows strong dominant body language, with his erect ears and staring eyes. It is *his* tail that flags stiffly out behind him, parallel to the ground—*not* the tail of the pup at the front left.

The pup at the front left displays totally submissive facial and body language: flattened ears; eyes closed down to slits; lips stretched back; and a bowed head. His tail is so far tucked beneath his body between his legs that it is difficult to see. He is not only instinctively protecting his genital area, he is actively submitting to the very packmate he seems to be charging.

The dynamic complexities of this form of play behavior will serve these pups well in the future when they join the adults in taking down prey. They can begin to compete for status—not necessarily alpha status—as early as four weeks old.

Succinctly put: play behavior in wolf pups is direct training for hunting behavior; direct training for making the kill.

As we follow the action of this two-frame sequence, once again the true story will be revealed.

Tag, You're It!

{ Young Canadian Timber Wolves }

SO NOW WE HAVE IT. The pup at the front right, who had given himself away with that solicitously raised paw, has assumed a passive demeanor, with the standard, ritualized flattened ears and squinty eyes of a subordinate.

The pup who had been at the rear left of the previous shot, and had shown all the dominant physical traits, continues his assertive behavior by being the one to carry the action to his packmate: he gently grabs the top of his head in his mouth.

The pup at the front left, who had been so submissive—although he had attempted to show some degree of assertiveness—comes toward his pack-mate from *below*. Given this type of personality profile, had this pup been alone with his packmate on the right, he most likely would have never attempted *any* assertive posturing. Here, he is psychologically reinforced by the presence of the other pups.

I have seen this behavior countless times not only in wolves, but also in packs of roaming street dogs, who may harass livestock, deer, or human be-ings. One or two dogs lead the pack in its everyday travels; the others fol-low, and are psychologically reinforced by the dominants.

This photo sequence helps bear out one of the few true generalizations that can be made about wolves: that they exhibit many different personalities.

Visage, Points Five

{ Adult Canadian Timber Wolf }

THIS SWEET-FACED CANADIAN MALE exhibits the special quality that I have long felt about the overall appearance of a mature wolf's head. That is, its resemblance to a five-pointed star: the point at the tip of each ear; the point of the nose; and the slightly tufted points at either end of the ruff.

If there were such a thing as a constellation of a wolf's face, I think it would have been chosen from such a handsome specimen.

Tactical

} Adult Canadian Timber Wolf {

READY FOR THE ATTACK, KIM displays a technique that wolves of mountainous regions have used to catch prey, for millions of years.

When hunting their prey—Dall sheep, bighorn sheep, or Rocky Mountain goats—wolves in Alaska's Interior, Canada's Northwest Territories (particularly the Mackenzie Delta), and the Rocky Mountains of the Canadian and American west have learned to split the pack into "teams," where several members will climb to the summit of a high slope, while the remainder of the pack waits below, sandwiching the prey between them.

When the moment of optimum advantage is at hand, the wolves will sweep down from above and drive the panicked prey straight toward the team that awaits below. As the two groups of predators converge, the prey—despite their great agility and nimble footing on rocky surfaces—are hard pressed to get away once their "escape routes" have been cut off.

There seems to be a common misconception by the public that wolves have a type of game plan when they chase prey; that they have *intellectually* devised a series of tactical maneuvers to take down their quarry.

In reality, wolves thrive by trial and error. They are virtual masters at adapting specific behaviors into everyday use, which they have learned by chance or by accident.

I saw no greater example of this concept—oddly enough—than on our educational wolf lecture tour, when "my boy," a jet-black Alaskan Timber wolf named Mori, having stood by my side in a hallway at Florida State University as we prepared to enter the lecture hall, watched me take a drink from a water fountain. The second I backed away from the fountain, Mori bunted his big front paws, once, twice, three times on the floor, then ceremoniously rose up, placed his left paw on the top of the machine to anchor himself, then placed his right paw squarely on the water fountain's silver plunger, and took his *own* drink.

I, of course, thought I'd entered the Twilight Zone. But the incident happened just as I have related it. Mori had watched me, watched me, and watched me. Then, whether he had literally figured out the process of taking his own drink, or if he was simply—but amazingly—imitating my actions, I am not certain to this day. All I know is that no drinking fountains were safe in the state of Florida, after that moment.

And as for Kim, in this photo her tactical charge was made on a beaver in a nearby pond. But it was *no lo contendo*. The beaver angrily slapped its tail on the surface of the water and swam away, leaving Kim nosing the snow-covered shoreline, as seen in the next image.

Lost Opportunities

{ Adult Canadian Timber Wolf }

AFTER HER CHARGE DOWN THE hill, Kim closely noses the shoreline for the scent of the beaver that got away. But she is not dwelling over her lost opportunities. She will catalogue the scent of the beaver in her brain, so that next time there will be an even more immediate recognition of the prey's close proximity.

Snacktime

AN ELDERLY FEMALE NIBBLES ON the severed femur bone of an elk. This behavior appears almost dainty, as her chiseled incisor teeth and worn canines are used to separate pieces of bone and sinew.

When wolves make a kill (which, with moose, is successful only about 7 percent of the time), they first consume the most nutritious organs, then the muscle mass and fat, and finally the fur and bone as well.

Wolves *do not* "hate" the animals they attack for food, just as we do not hate the chicken, steak, salad, or vegetables that we consume. Their aggressive behavior in hunting is geared only toward survival—which means employing all their physical and mental skills in the chase and "take-down."

In the wild, they may individually consume anywhere from five to twenty pounds of food at one time, the average meal being about ten pounds. Ninety to 95 percent of their diet is made up of meat, or some composition of meat, such as cartilage, fat, sinew, and bone. The remainder comes from the pre-digested vegetable matter within their prey's intestines.

This may sound disgusting to us, but it is nature's way of ensuring top condition for the pack leaders, and for the subordinates as well. Remember: various cultures of *our* species eat steak-and-kidney pie, braised liver, calves' brains, pig's feet, and goat eyeballs. Culinary delight, therefore, is in the taste of the beholder.

However, the popular belief that wolves regularly hunt and eat mice is quite erroneous. Arctic wolves can weigh ninety pounds and more for females, and well over one hundred pounds for males. Just *one* wolf of this size would need to spend many hours, catching anywhere from *twenty to sixty mice*, for *one meal*. Repeat this process for a pack of ten to thirteen wolves (as are the sizes of some Alaskan and High Canadian packs), and you have chaos—chaos, and a bunch of really exhausted wolves.

On a worldwide scale, scientists figure that mice comprise approximately 2 percent of the wolf's diet. Someone might argue that 2 percent can be a large individual total of mice, on a global scale. Perhaps—but this also means that *98 percent* of the wolf's diet is *not* mice.

An excellent living example of the predator-prey dynamic took place on Isle Royale, in Lake Superior off the coast of Michigan's Upper Peninsula, in 1972. Heavy snows that winter bogged down many moose. Wolves were then able to catch and kill them in much higher numbers than normal and with greater ease, dramatically dropping the moose population. In the following year, moose cows gave birth not to single calves as usual, but to *twin* calves, thus compensating for the previous year's losses.

Once again, nature, in its infinite wisdom, provided for both predator and prey alike.

One Paw Raised

{ Adolescent Canadian Timber Wolf }

MY CAMERA LENS CATCHES A magnificent young adult male as he stops still and stares in my direction. His slightly raised paw is the cue to two different conditions—one of concentration, and one of uncertainty, at that given moment.

I can just hear the thoughts running through his mind: *What* is that? Is it a threat? Am I in danger? Should I flee? Should I stay?

Alas, after a short while, the tranquil "teenager" simply placed his raised paw back on the ground and walked slowly away, over the snowy ridgeline of the hill.

The frame you see here was my favorite choice of a sequence that I had slowly fired off. It portrays the large wolf in his species' ultimate glory—a full winter coat, with a mustache-fringe of icicles hanging from his belly. His cold yellow eyes are perfectly framed by brushstroke markings of rich black, as if he were wearing mascara. His long plume tail extends beyond the hocks, or rear "elbow joints," of his legs.

Tragically, it is the luxuriant quality of their fine winter coats that has led to the deaths of millions of wolves. It takes the fur of *five* adult wolves just to make up one full-length wolf coat.

This practice began in earnest with the first wolf bounties in North America, in the year 1630, in Boston, Massachusetts.

THE CATHEDRAL HOWL

{ MIXED-GENDER ADULT WOLVES }

IT WAS ON AN IMPROMPTU visit to a wolf preserve in New York State, some years ago, that I came to a remarkable realization. As I stood watching a pair of packmates—one, female (left), the other, male (right)—a siren sounded in the not-too-far-off distance. The other members of the pack began lifting their muzzles toward the sky. By the luck of the Fates, the two subjects of this photo, without any visible signal, pitched their heads at nearly identical angles, forming a configuration that made me think of a church, or cathedral's steeple.

As I focused the telescopic lens of my camera, I discovered that both wolves were *curling back* the tips of their tongues, into their mouths, forming a sort of "sound-cone" that carried their voices far away. In the wild, this might be a message to alien packs or intruders to stay away.

Wolves, the "opera singers" of the wilderness.

Tag-Team

{ Mature Canadian Timber Wolves }

THIS FRAME FEATURES BUTCH AND SUNDANCE from *The Sentinels* and *A Single Purpose*. Here, like a tag-team in wrestling, they gang up on their rival pack member, displaying tall body postures, potent direct stares of the eyes, and erect ears and tails: classic wolf posture that says, "We are united against you; together, we are stronger than you; we are more dominant than you."

The pack member on the ground—at least for the moment—does not appear overly concerned about his present situation, or, for that matter, too intimidated by it. However, if you look closely at his face, you will see that his lips are stretched back in a subtle gesture that betrays his true uncertainty, and sense of submission, when challenged by *two* packmates at once.

Nothing dramatic developed from this encounter. The pack member on the lower right got to his feet and simply walked away. Butch and Sundance followed him a bit, then turned around and separated.

The irony, here, is that Butch and Sundance could only dominate their rival as a "team." When operating individually, the rival handily dominated each one of them. Just one more behavioral dynamic in the soap opera that is the life of the pack.

SALT AND PEPPER

{ MATURE ALASKAN TUNDRA WOLF }

FROM THE PLUMP DROPLET OF saliva that is about to plummet off her lower lip, to the blackest tips of her ears, this exquisite, pensive female shows the entire spectrum of shades and gradations that chronicle the aging process of the black-phase wolf.

Allow your eyes to wander over the surface of her muzzle, forehead, mask of her face, and length of her neck, and you will see every variation from black, gray, ash, charcoal, silver, to white.

To my mind, though, I prefer to keep it simple. I prefer to call her Salt and Pepper.

THREE FOR THE ROAD

{ MATURE HUDSON BAY WOLVES }

APPEARING LIKE A LUPINE VERSION of "I Love a Parade," these Hudson Bay wolves (whose habitat, a sort of low-level tundra, can be found in the Keewatin District of Canada) head north, across their territory, most likely in search of prey.

Wolves are ever the opportunists. Their well-honed survival skills drive them to take the path of least resistance. The single-file formation being used here is often employed in deep snows, where the lead wolf can clear a trail for the rest of the pack. The other members can then simply follow in the established footsteps as the most efficient mode of travel. But do not make the mistake of thinking that the wolf in the lead is automatically the pack leader. I have often seen the most dominant member of a wolf pack marching squarely in the middle of the pack's single-file configuration, like a quarterback in football at the helm of a scrimmage-line. From such a center vantage point, he is able to observe everything around him—and to respond quickly to any situation.

Sadly, though, for wolves, sometimes the "path of least resistance" can also be the path to death: because many of the open trails that wolves take—such as the one in this photo—are old or current logging roads, frequented by men with guns.

FATHER AND SON

{ MIXED-AGE CANADIAN TIMBER WOLVES }

TWO ROBUST MALES IN PRIME condition stop beneath the crisp, noonday winter sun to absorb its comforting warmth.

I strongly suspect that these two shared a father-son relationship, as the male on the left, with his broader head and lighter facial markings that come with the passage of years, was the only member of the large, seventeen-wolf pack at the correct age to have sired an adolescent son of about two years old.

Notice the son's darkly spired facial markings, narrower skull, and less developed, or "younger" expression.

As evidenced in this shot, these two males always hung out together, and explored their territory together.

All fathers and sons could take a lesson from a pair of wolves.

REFLECTIONS

WHEN I CAME UPON THIS lone female on a sun-drenched afternoon, she seemed to be reflecting on something off to her left, while at the same time her own image was mystically reflected in the ripples of water beneath her.

It struck me how, in the surreal world of the reflection, there are trees and branches and pine needles that cannot be seen in the real-world landscape above. There is such a harmony between the parallel realms represented here that they form a perfect matrix where the wolf's paw touches the lake's surface.

It is late May, and this female is in the process of "blowing her coat"— an expression used to describe the means by which a wolf's heavy, woolly undercoat (which can reach three inches thick) rises to the surface of the body, and is taken—or "blown" away—by the brisk northern winds. It is nature's "air-conditioning system" for heavily furred mammals, leaving them stripped down to the short, thin hairs of their topcoat, ready for the summer heat to come.

If you reach out and touch this image, you can almost *feel* the ringlets of water radiating toward you.

Full Speed Ahead!

{ Adult Canadian Timber Wolf }

A DETERMINED MALE PACK MEMBER slices through a narrow channel, cutting inverted Vs into the surface of the water with his long, wedge-shaped muzzle. Ironically, the very same inverted Vs were created by the sharply angled bow of my aluminum freighting canoe, the two forming a strange, timeless parallel between human and beast.

Wolves are excellent swimmers, and will spread their flexible webbed paws wide like paddles, to propel themselves for miles. Despite these impressive capabilities, their larger and stronger prey (moose, deer, caribou) are often able to escape them in the water, because *they* are even stronger swimmers than their wolf pursuers.

Over the decades, I've come to realize that this photo may be one of the rarest images of a wolf ever taken. Out of some one hundred and fifty books on the species published since the mid-1940s, there have been many images of wolves in the water, but very few, to the best of my knowledge, of a wolf *actually swimming*.

In the Pink

{ Adult Canadian Timber Wolf }

THE PERFECT, PEACEFUL EXPRESSION ON this mature male's face shows a wolf in the prime of life and the prime of health. He stares out at something unknown to me, in the distance.

Because wolves do not see color in the precise way we do, they do not perceive the full spectrum of primary colors, like red. They do, however, see some diluted form of it (based on scientific research of the 1970s).

Unlike human vision, which is based on fields of "rods" and "cones," wolves possess only rod vision. It is cone vision that allows human beings to perceive the full spectrum of colors.

ANGST

{ MATURE CANADIAN TIMBER WOLVES }

IN THIS PRELUDE TO THE next image, Butch's nemesis has driven him down to the water's edge. The body language and physical displays say it all: Butch is in for a rough time; the aggressive pack member is throwing him an all-out direct stare. And all Butch can do is flash his teeth defiantly, then turn his gaze away from such an unyielding challenge.

I must admit to feeling sorry for Butch, and the undue angst he had to endure. But his rival—who was also a general troublemaker in the pack—eventually got what he deserved. For on a tranquil spring afternoon, when nothing in particular was happening, Butch's rival decided to disrupt the harmony of the pack, by picking on several of the male members.

Big mistake.

The former pack leader—a rather large individual—came careening over the crest of the centrally located hill that you see in many of the images in this book. He galloped down the hill's south slope like a runaway freight train and launched himself through the air, landed onto the troublemaker, then literally flipped him upside down, and seized his throat between his jaws. He did not kill Butch's nemesis, but used this severe physical intimidation to punish him, to strongly put him in his place, so that pack harmony would be restored. It was.

Wolves are usually loath to kill each other, except when a pack's territory has been invaded by an alien wolf, which potentially threatens the entire family. And after the psychological assault by the pack's former leader, Butch's rival then had to suffer his own angst. I suspect, though, that had he continued to harass and physically scar his fellow wolves, he might have well been "removed."

Cornered

{ Mature Canadian Timber Wolves }

BUTCH AND HIS RIVAL HAVE now taken their angst-filled antics into the water's shallows. The behavioral dynamics here are identical to the previous shot. Butch puts on a savage-looking, defensive display, while his assertive packmate shoots him that rock-hard direct stare. He also displays very erect ears, a raised, flagging tail, and the puckered corners of his lips, that more than suggest he is growling.

I find it interesting that, theoretically, Butch could have used the entire expanse of water behind him to make his escape, yet he still looks trapped, still looks "cornered."

But come to think of it, there was really nowhere for Butch to go. If he had attempted to swim away, his antagonist could have swum after him. And he was in no position to get past the other wolf on foot without being heavily chased.

So, what was the outcome of this little meeting of the minds?

Well, Butch may have been submissive, but he was certainly no dummy. He simply waited out his rival, and eventually walked away, using what I like to think of as the "Mahatma Gandhi Defense." However, the next time they met, Butch had his buddy Sundance by his side. The outcome, as you can imagine, was somewhat different.

Chorus

LOOKING LIKE A SEVENTEENTH-CENTURY explorer's nightmare, this pack blends its voices in unison. The belief that wolves howl at the moon most likely arose in North America from sightings of whole packs gathered at hilltops beneath the illuminating glow of a full moon. Other times, it would have been too dark to observe this primordial wilderness ritual.

It is quite possible that wolves instinctively choose clear, moonlit nights—when the air is free of sound-deadening clouds—to converge at hilltops, because under these conditions, their voices can carry the farthest distances and achieve the most efficient results for declaring territory, or for simply expressing joyful sentiments.

What makes this image so unique for me is that it serves as a virtual blueprint for studying wolf-howling dynamics. Each wolf has become part of a subgroup in the pack. Even the position of each member's mouth can be bisected with a line, running between his or her opened lips, down past the corners.

These subgroups have formed a kind of fan structure that not only helps blend the variations and subtle nuances of each wolf's voice into a solid, droning wall of sound, but also strengthens the message of the joint howl in every direction.

There will be no mistake made—no room for error from any alien species—that *this* territory is definitely occupied.

The chorus has done its job well.

Ahead by a Nose

⹂ Canadian Timber Wolf ⹂

WHILE LECTURING ON BEHALF of the Wild Canid Survival and Research Center in St. Louis—Jalene, my first lecture wolf, took it upon herself to "excavate" a lovely, deep bed—a ditch—in the corner of a friend's backyard. At first, I panicked a bit when I did not see her standing or lying along the ground, as any wolf would normally do. But on closer inspection, I saw what is presented here in this image: a gentle, pointy-eared wolf face, totally content, dramatically punctuated by that wide-nostriled, jet-black nose. In all, both a comical and clever sight.

Even at the tender age of six months, Jalene had instinctively fashioned a bit of privacy and shelter for herself by plopping down between the earthen walls of her four-foot-deep makeshift home.

It is precisely this type of independent action propelled by instinct and determination that has allowed wolves to survive for two million years in North America.

Whenever I'm about to say to myself, "Wolves cannot do this," or "They cannot accomplish that," they then prove me wrong by doing it.

After you've watched a wolf float through the air over the back of its packmate, or jump ten feet straight up from a sitting position, or crush bone with one bite of its molar teeth, you then appreciate that they move like liquid fur and are made of instinct and energy.

What's Up?

TWO PUPS (LEFT), APPROXIMATELY FIVE months old, come over to investigate something of interest that their littermate (center) is protecting with a decidedly nasty snarl, which cannot easily be seen behind a tall flower.

The setting is a classic "rendezvous site"—an area usually chosen for its proximity to water and protected by trees, where pups between the ages of four to six months can play with one another, and where adult members of the pack act as "babysitters."

When the pups are six months old, they are grown enough to go out hunting with the pack as a whole. But they will not become fully skilled predators until they are approximately two years old, when they are sexually mature, and when they have learned most of the techniques of hunting prey from their elders.

Generations

THE CONTRAST BETWEEN THIS ROBUST pup (rear) at approximately six months old and this absolutely stunning adult male can easily be seen in this generational portrait.

Once more, I'm drawn to the tranquility of the moment, when the wolves are passive, yet alert, and not being subjected to the stresses of survival, or social interactions.

As the American poet Walt Whitman said, "They are so placid and self-contained." Perhaps he was he pointing out the simple fact that wild animals do not need us to survive. They do not depend upon us for their happiness. They eat when they are hungry. They sleep when they are tired. And, like us, they give birth, feel pain, express joy, struggle to survive, and eventually die.

If we care at all about saving wolves, we need only gaze into the two faces in this photo, to know that we should not save them because they are physically beautiful, or because they are highly intelligent, or even because they are similar to humans in many ways. If we are to save wolves, it should be for the sole reason that they exist, and because they have a basic right to live in peace, on this planet.

BLACKWATCH

{ MATURE ALASKAN TUNDRA WOLF }

LOOK INTO THE VISAGE OF this spectacular black-phase female and you will know why the ancient Romans chose the wolf as the symbol of their empire.

Even in the medium of black-and-white photography, one gets a sense of the power in those sulphur-yellow eyes.

For me, black wolves are the most mystical creatures of the universe—their rich, dark faces, ominously punctuated by deep, moon-set orbs. And when combined with the angular, pointed features of their ears, muzzles, and layered ruffs, the result is something positively primitive. So primitive, in fact, that in Medieval Europe—particularly France—it was believed that a male wolf with yellow eyes could seduce a woman simply by staring at her.

Since all wolves get lighter in color (or shading) as they get older—perhaps most prominently noticed in the black-phase wolves—this specific female's transformation shows itself in even brushstrokes of silver on her cheeks and forehead, and white around her chin and point of her muzzle.

It would not be improbable to observe a jet-black wolf at six months old, then go away, and come back years later to see a silver or white animal—the *same* animal—in its place.

Don't Look At Me—I'm Naked!

{ Adult Alaskan Tundra Wolf }

IT'S MIDSUMMER, AND THIS SWEET-LOOKING Alaskan female is totally devoid of her thick winter coat. Or, bluntly put, she is "naked."

Her ruff is so depleted that you can see the gaps—like cardboard cutouts—where there used to be fur, at each side of the top of her neck.

Her eyes are so big, intense, and expressive, that she almost seems to be self-conscious about her "bare condition."

But give it three months, and she'll be fully clothed once again.

BONDING

A LOWER-RANKING MALE (STANDING) GREETS the leader of the pack with a well-received offering of affection.

This type of interaction between wolves provides a moment of calm reassurance that helps reduce potential or existing pack tensions, and serves to psychologically bond the members to one another for the trials and tribulations of everyday survival.

Although the subordinate's tail is raised, it is flagging from side to side. An erect, or raised tail, in wolf body language, does not automatically indicate a high-status animal. It can represent a whole range of emotions, from "I'm interested in what's going on" to "I'm happy" to "I'm agitated" to "I want to play."

If only human beings had tails that they could raise and lower, shift from side to side, or tuck between their legs. . . . Things might run more smoothly in our lives.

Hail to the Chief

{ Adult Canadian Timber Wolves }

THE BEHAVIORAL DYNAMIC CAPTURED IN this image separates it from other greeting rituals that have preceded it in *Wolf Empire*. To my mind, this is the most important greeting ritual of all.

A pack gathering brings many, if not all of the pack's members around the alpha, where they will nuzzle and lick, squeak and whine, and physically rub their bodies against him in a grand gesture of not only respect but often also of solicitation—an urging for the pack to go on the hunt.

This, to me, is the alpha's crowning moment. He stands proud and tall, as he benevolently absorbs the shower of "love and affection" from an adoring family, some of whom might be carrying the scent of recently discovered prey on their bodies.

But my absolutely favorite type of pack gathering ritual is the kind that morphs into a joyous, boisterous, droning howl, as seen in *Chorus*.

I think one of the greatest gifts that wolves have given me is their amazing capacity for enjoying life. Once you've experienced an uninhibited, exuberant, raucous wolf gathering and pack howl, you will learn what it is to be truly alive.

Bodacious
and Reinforcements

{ Alaskan Timber Wolves }

THESE TWO PHOTOGRAPHS TOOK SEVEN rolls of film to capture. I knew what type of image I wanted before I went out to photograph for the day—a very Zen thing shared by a good number of professional photographers. And I knew that I could eventually get the shot. But by the time I reached my 250th frame, with only two left to go, my usual patience had run out. I was so exasperated that I plopped my rear-end down on the shallow slope I'd been standing on, and let go a string of expletives that violated the primary rules of the forest: first, make no noise; and second, leave nature the same way that you entered it.

But the wolf gods were with me that hot and humid afternoon. The black pup (whom I estimate to have been about eight weeks old) suddenly popped out from behind his protective boulder, showing the audacity of his youth, and the ever-present curiosity of his kind. I quickly snapped the picture.

So there I was, with one shot left, and my instincts telling me to wait—wait for something *else* to happen. And it did. The black pup backed up, as its slightly smaller littermate (whom I suspect was a female) came forward, sporting her lopsided left ear.

It was at that moment I realized just *how much* wolves make use of the natural landmarks around them to create a sense of security for themselves. I also discovered why I had gone through seven rolls of film to reach these last two frames. For if you look beyond the black pup, you will see their mother warily peeking out at me from the safety of her boulder. She had kept her babies hidden the entire afternoon, but when her son disobeyed her and popped into view—thereby instigating his sister's rebellion—her maternal instincts got the better of her. She, too, was compelled to expose herself to potential danger—a thought that saddened me when finally, the three wolves dashed into the underbrush and out of sight.

Snowflakes

{ Adolescent Alaskan Tundra Wolf }

I LOVE THIS IMAGE FOR its peaceful contrast to our increasingly violent global society.

Although wolves are beasts of great power, stealth, and vitality, they possess a skill that we are rapidly losing, which is the ability to stop, rest, and shut out the poisons of the world around them. For wolves, though, the only true poison is humankind.

Just looking at this contented male makes me wonder: What are you thinking? What do you *really* see behind those tightly closed eyes of yours?

After many years spent with wolves, I feel that I know what they might say to us, if they could speak. They would say, "Leave us to the wilderness. Leave us to eat. Leave us to sleep. Leave us to run and jump, to howl and make love; to play and sniff the night air.

"But most of all: Leave us alone."

SOUNDWATCH

{ Mature Alaskan Timber Wolf }

BALANCING HERSELF ALONG THE EDGE of a tiny rock promontory, the elegant female from *Salt and Pepper* listens to, then intently watches a flight of honking Canada geese.

Though wolves are commonly thought to possess an acute sense of smell and keen eyesight, these senses do not compare with their sense of hearing.

Adult wolves can hear the howl of another wolf up to six miles in the distance in the wild. They hear sounds *below* 250 cycles per second, about as well as human beings do. But wolves detect sonic levels *above* 250 cycles per second far better than human beings. And they have the ability to receive sonic vibrations, up to 26,000 cycles per second. Compare these numbers to the soft beating of a low, bass drum (350 cycles per second) or a dog whistle on high-pitch or silent mode (18,000 cycles per second), which is beyond human range.

I cannot count the times that even while my lecture wolves were curled up in a ball, sound asleep, their short, triangular ears rotated back and forth, like radar dishes on Navy destroyers—listening, listening.

Wolves are rarely, if ever, out of touch with the world of sound.

Reversal

I LOVE THIS IMAGE FOR its pure statement that few things in life are certain. When asked, "Which is the male wolf in this photo, and which is the female?" approximately 90 percent of viewers said that the pack member on the right was the male.

Wrong.

In an interesting reversal of the laws of "sexual dimorphism," the wolf on the left, with his slender build, soft eyes, and quirky smile, is the male of the two. The petite, but robust, fully furred creature, with the broad head and well-developed ruff, is the female. When it comes to wolves, the laws of individuality take precedence over the laws of sexual dimorphism.

I'm certain of it.

JUST A GIRL

ALTHOUGH I ALWAYS STRIVE TO keep my wolf-human comparisons down to a minimum, what can I say about the admittedly sweet, feminine expression on this petite female's face?

To me, she's just a girl.

Survivor

{ Adult Canadian Timber Wolf }

THIS IS ONE OF THOSE images that affects me on a very personal level.

Believe it or not, the subject of this photo is the same petite beauty seen in the previous picture, ten years later.

I came back to see her alive and thriving at approximately twelve or thirteen years old, but totally devoid of any facial markings. Her coat had turned from a rich buff hue with black overlays, to a pale biscuit hue with diluted black overlays.

Those sweet, expressive, oblique eyes had now turned to partly clouded, slightly rounded, slightly drooped eyes. But her "wolf soul"—her personal essence, if you will—was still intact. She had survived the deaths of several of her packmates from disease and old age.

However, one aspect of this photo brings a smile of amusement to my face: her slightly spread paw beneath the surface of the water—as seen in *Reflections*.

After I captured this image, I never saw "Just a Girl" again.

Take That!

{ Mature Canadian Timber Wolves }

THE MOMENTARY DISAGREEMENT THAT BROKE out in this scene was the direct result of my part-time experiments with wolves' sense of smell. Before these packmates ever arrived, I had laced several snowballs with Chanel No. 5 perfume, then tossed them across to the snow-covered hill opposite me.

Wolves love all kinds of pungent odors, so much so that they will become possessive over them. Here, a small female, at the top of the frame (center right), lashes out at a male member of the pack, after both tried to control the "perfumed" area.

Although the wolves on the periphery of this gathering show little real concern for the dispute, there is a fascinating behavioral dynamic at work here. The wolf in the foreground (center) appears nonchalant, as he noses the hillside. On closer inspection, though, his hackles are raised from the back of his head, down past his shoulders, and his tail is arched, or crooked, at its base.

This ability of wolves to subtly express a duality of emotion is proof of the great complexities in the species. For although the pack member in the foreground appears to be cool, calm, and collected, his physical displays are actually saying that he is somewhat agitated, or disturbed by the event.

Several times over the years, I have seen wolves in amazing role reversals, where the lowest omegas of the pack actually *backed down* the most dominant alphas over objects of possession ranging from the leg bone of a deer, to a stick, to access to a favored drinking site. And now, in the annals of wolfdom, to Chanel No. 5.

Tool-User

{ Mature Canadian Timber Wolf }

FOR DECADES NOW, ANTHROPOLOGISTS HAVE been telling us how primates and our earliest ancestors used tools to further their survival skills. Chimpanzees use long sticks to extract termites and grubs from their shelters. Early humans learned the secrets of fire. But here, in this fascinating moment, a clever female pack member quite intentionally raises herself and her line of sight by stepping onto a smooth rock outcrop, in order to track the movements of two deer in the distance.

This behavior had never been initiated by any other wolf in the Canadian pack. They were always gathering at the highest point of their territory to observe their world, but this was the first time that any of them quite deliberately made use of an object to get even higher, in order to produce a positive result that would aid in her survival. The rock outcrop was employed as a "mechanism" to directly increase the female's ability to spot prey or potential threats—more so than on a usual, daily basis.

Wolves—tool-users of the wilderness.

154

Tailgating

{ Adult Canadian Timber Wolves }

THE RATHER PETITE ALPHA FEMALE of the pack (left) comes up hard on the rear of a subordinate female during a playful scramble across their territory.

Wolves take great joy in play, and engage in it at any age, at any given moment. It serves as an important mechanism for reducing pack tensions. It helps tighten pack bonds between individuals, and is used as a training device for pups to learn hunting skills. Their running, lunging, biting, nipping, ambushing, and retreating behaviors are identical to adult hunting techniques.

Due to this fact, I have never encouraged play behavior between myself and the lecture wolves that I have raised since puppyhood. I've always suppressed those specific, potentially troublesome instincts that could ruin an educational program, especially on stage.

Alley-oop!!

MY CAMERA'S LENS CATCHES A rare moment: An agile male leaps onto the boulder at the heart of the pack's territory and surprises a female pack member.

He is actually seven-eighths in the air, as his front paws touch down on the rock cliff.

Wolves have been observed leaping fifteen feet across an open area in pursuit of prey. I have witnessed them jumping eight to ten feet straight up, from a sitting position, as though they had springboards in their feet. When you see such a sight, your immediate response is, "*Huh*?" Your second response is, "I wish *I* could do that."

But as consummate predators, they can run at a top speed of forty miles per hour, for short distances. And they can travel at a four to six mile per hour pace, for sixty miles or half a day, without stopping.

I wish I could do *that*, too.

SOLACE

DEEP IN THE HEART OF their territory, a mated pair (the male asleep, the female standing alertly) take in a quiet summer afternoon while their contented pup (far left, approximately four months old) seems to be gazing in the same direction as his mother.

This prominent flat-topped boulder served as a focal point for many of the pack's daily activities: play, disputes, rest and relaxation, family gatherings, and howling rituals.

But no activity gained my appreciation more than the sight of a single wolf lying outstretched on the boulder in a ray of sunlight.

Now *that's* solace.

THE GREETING

{ MATURE CANADIAN TIMBER WOLVES }

ENGAGED IN TEXTBOOK BEHAVIORAL DYNAMICS, the older male (left) displays the flattened ears and pulled-back lips of a friendly, submissive greeting. The wolf on the right stands with a tall, dominant posture and high-status tail as he receives the social gesture.

What I find most touching about this photo, however, is its unique backstory. The older male, the father of the other wolves in this photo, is actually submitting to one of them. But he was not only their father, he was also their pack leader—the same wolf blissfully asleep in *Serenity*. I was present to witness the sad demise of his role in the pack, when one overcast afternoon in January, three of his sons challenged him, nearly simultaneously, in an effort to support "Cary Grant" as the new pack leader.

At first, the elder male triumphed over each son by physically dominating him. But when Cary came in for the second hard challenge, and his brothers who were intent on defeating their father backed him up, the patriarch no longer had the strength to fight off three adult males at once. He was cast down onto the snow, belly-up, vanquished, and soon plummeted from his alpha status to near omega.

My heart wept for this indomitable and regal wolf—to see him fall so low like great Julius Caesar after his assassination. However, unlike mighty Caesar, the father-wolf rose slowly in status, back up through the ranks of the pack. Three years later, he had risen to the position of a "beta" wolf—a strong number two.

Eventually he rose to alpha again—an amazing feat to my mind—only to be once more usurped by his son. Yet even then, he served as a sort of "shop-steward" or "foreman" for the pack, using his wisdom to help make decisions for the benefit of all.

The image captured here shows the elder male when he has risen to the level of mid-ranking wolf. For me, though, the beauty of this anecdote is that he managed to live to a ripe old age of more than ten years—this is where we find him in *Serenity*.

He had been a king and had fallen from grace. Like Arthur of Camelot, through his knowledge, experience, and determination, he came to reign over his subjects for a brief moment in the sun once again.

Walk on By

IN A QUIET MOMENT ABOUT three hours after a snowfall, one of the male members of the Canadian pack calmly passes the center of activity.

Notice how each wolf is looking in a different direction. Although wolves are potent predators, they are also always on guard for potential threats from rival species.

Notice, too, the classic walking gait of the male in the foreground. He nearly touches his front left paw to his reaching rear right paw, as they converge toward an imaginary centerline; while his front right paw and rear left paw simultaneously stretch in opposite directions, to provide locomotion.

So, wolves use a combination of driving forces while balancing their weight directly beneath a central point of their bodies, setting up a type of "fulcrum" to support their overall length.

As ever, to be a wolf is to be efficient.

RELIEF

{ MATURE CANADIAN TIMBER WOLF }

AS MUCH AS I AM loath to make the comparison, this preoccupied young adult male reminds me of the average family dog seeking relief in the comfort of a good scratch.

The thick lining of fur in wolves' ears not only protects them from extreme cold and heat—as pointed out in the next image and in *Conserving Heat*—but also helps keep parasites such as mites, along with the ever-present blackflies and mosquitoes, out of their inner ears (which, of course, helps prevent infection).

Functionality aside, I broke into a big grin when I heard this lone pack member moaning and groaning like a "domestic-dog-of-satisfaction."

Fur-Ellipse

{ Mature Canadian Timber Wolf }

THE FIRST IMPRESSION I HAVE of this image is the perfect ellipse that this pack member has curled himself into. My second impression is, as always with wolves, their innate ability for conforming their bodies into parallel lines and themes.

This mature male's eye slits, left ear, cheek lines, and exposed front paw all approximate a forty-five-degree angle, while the curved top line of his back, expanse of his upper-thigh muscle, and scimitar-like tail all reach a uniform elliptical configuration—producing an intensely efficient and self-contained defense against the cold.

Perhaps no man is an island, but I'll wager that any wolf may become one.

PREPARATION

{ MATURE CANADIAN TIMBER WOLVES }

TWO OUT OF THREE WOLVES can't be wrong! Well, at least the members of this pack may think so, as the alpha female (front, left), and alpha male (center) curl themselves snugly into furred balls beneath the gathering gloom of night, and an approaching storm.

Their packmate at the far right does not seem to share their concern for the potential three feet of snow, sixty-five-mile-per-hour winds, and temperature plunges to far below zero Fahrenheit. Or at least he has not yet committed himself to the notion.

I have always found it a wondrous sight when coming upon my Alaskan malamute sled dogs covered over by snow, or seeing wolves in the guise of snowy mounds, dappling the forest landscape.

When wolves are curled into a ball—as in this image—and grouped closely together, their collective body heat helps keep each of them warm. But when falling snow blankets the hollow strands of their fur, a layer of oxygen is formed or trapped between the surface of their coats and the snow, which also helps to preserve body heat.

It's time for the pack member on the far right to "get with the program."

Morning Stroll

{ MATURE CANADIAN TIMBER WOLF }

HIS HEAD LOWERED IN TYPICAL wolf fashion, this undaunted male walks calmly through his pack's territory, after a fresh snow has fallen the night before.

The overall appearance of the wolf's hunched shoulders, angled head, and piercing yellow eyes has, in folklore and myth, been interpreted by superstitious, uneducated people to signify evil, cunning, or treachery. The reality is that this wolf is doing nothing more than traversing a favored hillside, minding his own business.

Wolves often lower their heads in order to see better through branches, over large rocks and bushes, or to focus on objects in the distance.

It is purely a physiological behavior, not a pact with the Devil.

Peekaboo

{ MATURE CANADIAN TIMBER WOLF }

I CAPTURED THIS IMAGE ON a truly dark, gloomy day, sitting atop a snowy embankment, while my rear end became increasingly wet. But my efforts were rewarded, when this pretty, petite female appeared from the ridgeline across from me and hopped up onto the prominent flat-topped boulder. Because of my work with our lecture wolves, I could easily estimate that she stood approximately twenty-five inches tall at the shoulders and weighed about sixty-five pounds.

The sense of security created by the dead pine tree beside her allowed her the courage to peek out at me from behind its tall trunk.

Sadly, it is this same irresistible sense of curiosity that has led to the death of so many wolves over the centuries. Or, as I prefer to say, "Curiosity didn't kill the cat. Curiosity killed the wolf."

The Veteran

{ Adult Alaskan Timber Wolf }

THIS DISTINGUISHED OLDER MALE IS undoubtedly the largest wolf I've ever seen. He was the size of a Great Dane. But what I appreciated most about him—as I took his picture from no more than thirty feet away in a large wolf preserve in Virginia—was that he was also one of the mellowest wolves I'd ever met.

I estimated that he stood about thirty-two inches tall at the shoulders, and weighed approximately one hundred and twenty pounds.

It still never fails to intrigue me that this robust silver and charcoal elder, with his time-bleached face and dark highlights, was at one time as black as blackest night.

Low Bridge

{ Adult Canadian Timber Wolf }

THE HANDSOME PACK LEADER I'VE nicknamed "Cary Grant"/"George Clooney," in a somewhat less than dignified moment, pokes his head out from beneath the belly of an elderly female—most likely, his mother.

Notice how age has shaped the appearance of each animal. The younger male retains his vibrant facial markings—the "spires" beneath his eyes, and the broad nasal bar that descends his muzzle to his nose. In contrast, the old female is totally devoid of facial markings and displays a faded nasal bar.

No one said that growing old was any fun. But this matriarch has managed to maintain her dignity.

The Living Werewolf

{ Mature Alaskan Timber Wolf }

I HAVE COME TO CONSIDER this photo the rarest photo of a wolf ever taken. Your brain is basically processing an image—a wolf standing bipedally like a human being—that should not exist in nature.

The animal in this frame was in no way photographically, digitally, or behaviorally altered. I know because she was my own wolf, Raven, with whom I did many educational lectures, television shows, and public appearances. As I have always stressed, *none* of the lecture wolves that I worked with was a pet. They were very special, individual creatures and invaluable educational tools, who from a very young age distinguished themselves from other members of their species by showing little to no stress in the presence of human beings.

This image is actually the second frame in a series of three in which I photographed Raven in a snowstorm, in her spacious enclosure. The first frame of the sequence captures her giving me a solicitous "play-bow." Her head is cocked back over her shoulder. She's squinty eyed, and grinning coquettishly. Her body posture— chest bowed low, rear end up in the air—is saying, "C'mon. Come play with me. " The third frame of the sequence shows Raven in the air, in flight. The bottoms of her feet hang several inches above my six-foot-tall frame, as she leaps for joy.

I chose *not* to include the first and third images, here, because I felt they would detract from this second frame's amazing qualities. I've come to realize, now, that I will most likely never see an image of a wolf like this one, ever again.

THE LONESOME TRAIL

{ ADULT HUDSON BAY WOLF }

OF ALL THE IMAGES I've taken over the years, this one touches me most deeply. It speaks to that organic isolation we all feel at one time or another, and creates a vision in our mind's eye of the challenges before us on the road of life.

This robust specimen of a Hudson Bay wolf may have been part of a pack, or he may have been a member of that exclusive wolf club known as "lone wolves."

The lone wolf is one of the most romantic images associated with the species. As many as 28 percent of all wolf sightings prove to be true loners. In the 1940s, scientists believed that lone wolves were old males or females whose mates had died. Quite often, these older wolves may keep to themselves and no longer take part in pack outings or important social rituals. They drift away from the pack, until eventually they become separated by hours, then days, then weeks. Elderly wolves who lose vital teeth can no longer take part in the hunt for food. Here again, their lack of involvement in such important parts of wolf existence separates them from everyday pack life.

Lone wolves were once thought to be low-ranking individuals who were ostracized by the pack to the point of being driven out of their territory. Any attempts to get back in the pack's good graces would open them up to being chased or physically harassed.

It was also believed that old pack leaders who had been challenged by younger pack members and defeated were then forced out of the pack. But quite often, former pack leaders are actually *cared for* by the rest of the pack—even though they may no longer lead the hunt or bring new life in the form of pups.

In more recent years, lone wolves have been given a new status as individuals who are born with naturally dominant personalities, and who back down least in the serious physical interactions between pack members. By age two—when they become sexually mature—they may challenge the pack leader. If defeated, they may leave the pack to find a lone wolf of the opposite sex, with whom to start their own new pack and create fresh wolf bloodlines.

It is most likely, though, that *all* of these "lone wolf" theories are valid. Yet, unlike our own kind, loners do not act out or behave in aberrant ways. Wolves have shown me, in thirty-five years, that there are creatures who walk this Earth who do not grasp for personal power out of greed, self-righteousness, or an attempt to force a personal agenda on others. To my mind, they are more "noble" than their human counterparts; more aware of their surroundings, and more in touch with their limitations among the elements of nature.

Afterword

I HAVE BEEN FORTUNATE ENOUGH to walk among wolves in the Canadian forests; to enter a world that remains unchanged for millennia—an ancient, timeless, and primitive realm where one slip from a small rock ledge can end in your death. This is wilderness, and this is the measure of wolves as a species: to be born, struggle to survive, feel pain, express joy, and eventually die.

There are important lessons to be learned from wolves; lessons that I strive to incorporate into my daily life; lessons that only a creature who thrives on instinct and energy could teach us.

First, feel no guilt. This does not mean forget about the wrongs you commit. It means, do not dwell on that which you cannot control, or that which you must do to survive. The wolf does not feel guilty for taking down the baby moose or elderly doe. It simply hunts, kills, and feeds, to carry on. There is no guilt; there is no remorse. There is no disdain.

Second, have fun. Do not be afraid to make a fool of yourself. Do not be afraid to be silly. Do not think that you are so important that you cannot allow yourself the right to be a child again. The wolf I photographed in *Ecstasy* taught me this.

Third, to gain some degree of control over your life, you must give up control, as I learned from the former alpha in *The Greeting*. When the time is right, the possession of that control will come back to you. It will be yours again.

Fourth, when you love, love to the utmost of your ability. Love unselfishly. Love with respect. Love with devotion. For that which we call love can be snatched away from us in the blink of an eye.

Finally, there is no equalizer greater than death. Share the best of yourself with your friends, with your family, with strangers. And know that you belong to something larger than yourself—the "global pack," the human family. For when you fail—and you will fail—there will be others around to help pick you up. There will be others to say, "Yes, I have been there too."

All these things I have seen in wolves.

Now, as we end our journey through these pages together, I leave you with a wish, with a hope: that this book has given you new knowledge and a new appreciation for the one creature that is, in many ways, "more human than humans"—at least by the highest standards *we* set for ourselves.

And as for me, I await the day, the hour, the very moment that I may take my first footsteps back . . . back into the wolf empire.